MW00439632

The Stolen Dog

TRICIA O'MALLEY

The Stolen Dog
Copyright © 2013 by Tricia O'Malley
All Rights Reserved

Copyeditor: Carrie Lauer
Cover Design: Josh O'Malley

All rights reserved. This book was self-published by the author Tricia O'Malley under Park & Stowell Publishing. No part of this book may be reproduced in any form by any means without express permission of the author. This includes reprints, excerpts, photocopying, recording, or any future means of reproducing text.

If you would like to do any of the above, please seek permission first by contacting the author at: www.thestolendog.com.

Published in the United States by Park & Stowell Publishing.
ISBN 978-0-9894351-1-6

*For **Tante Jo** — who followed her own path, saving animals and humans alike, all while sharing laughter through her tattered joke book.*

"Until one has loved an animal, a part of one's soul remains unawakened."

— *Anatole France*

Words from the Author

The story of Briggs has served as inspiration to many. From making others better dog parents to reminding us to pay attention to others that need help, Briggs' story has touched many. To this day, we continue to help others whose dogs are lost or stolen. At www.thestolendog.com, you'll find our guide to mobilizing a movement of people who will care about your lost or stolen animal. Even better, a portion of the proceeds from the sale of this book will be donated to shelters and rescues. In this way, Briggs' story will continue to help other animals in need.

Acknowledgements

Josh, my rock, I thank you for your unwavering support and your inherent knack for teasing a smile from me no matter the situation. This was our story and I am humbled that you let me share it.

To our friends and family, those mentioned in the book and those not, without you Briggs would not be home, nor would this story have come to fruition. Josh and I thank all of you for your continued support and friendship.

To the community as a whole, there are no words to appropriately thank you for your help. Every social media share, every flyer printed, every Briggs sighting reported culminated in a collective powerful energy that forced this man to return Briggs. This is your story, too.

That Day

I AM CONVINCED THAT THE phone sounds different when there is bad news on the other end. It's as if the pitch of the ring shifts ever so slightly. My husband's picture flashed across the screen.

Somehow I already knew this was not an "I'm thinking about you," or "how's your day going," kind of call.

"Briggs is gone!" Josh shouted into the phone, speaking of our two-year-old sassy, stinky, laughable Boston terrier, a central focus of our lives.

"What!? What do you mean?" Confused, I scribbled down everything he was saying, my words chaotically strewn across a pink Post-it note. The note's cheerfulness battled in vain with the terrifying words it held.

"I left him on the deck while I went inside to change. I had this really bad feeling so I ran back downstairs…and he was gone!" Josh's voice scratched through the phone as if he were willing the words to be untrue.

"Okay, okay. Calm down. He clearly must have gotten out of the fence somehow. Just run down the alley and call for him. You know he never runs far. You'll find him, honey. Just go!"

This was a time for action, not words, and Josh hung up. I stared at the phone with intensity, hoping that I could use some manner of Jedi mind tricks to lead Josh to Briggs. Within ten minutes Josh called back. Increasingly panicked, his words were fractured by gulps of air. The sound of his feet pounding on the pavement echoed his panic through the phone.

"He's not here — he's just gone! I can't find him!"

"Just keep looking!" I said, my chest tightening as bands of fear snaked through me. I slammed my laptop closed, the fluorescent light piercing my eyes, as I rushed to tell the office manager that I had to leave.

I had to go.

As I raced home, numbness crept through me. The beating of my heart amplified in my ears, silencing the everyday sounds of traffic that flitted by my open window.

Somehow, I knew. I don't know how, but I just knew.

Briggs was stolen.

With a complete disregard for safety, I raced through several red lights and reached our neighborhood in record time. I slowed down, my eyes blurry as I desperately scanned the yards and alleyways, praying for a glimpse of black and white. I startled strangers on the street, screaming to them from my open window, "Hey you! Have you seen a Boston terrier?"

My thoughts were at war with each other, tumbling, tripping, and falling all over themselves. Yet a consistent theme emerged.

Help. Please. Help us. Help me. Briggs. Briggs. Please help him.

The spring day laughed at me as I squealed to a stop in front of our house. Our neighborhood was disgustingly picturesque. Sunlight filtered through the leaves while stay-at-home moms pushed their peaceful babies in strollers.

I was the chaos in this otherwise heavenly little slice of Americana.

Josh clattered down our front steps, panic radiating from him. Sweat dripped from his clean-shaven head, and his pale Irish skin was flushed from sprinting around the neighborhood. He climbed into the car and slammed the passenger door with a ferocity that mirrored his disheveled appearance. Panting, he looked at me, his warm brown eyes terror-stricken.

"Go!" he said.

Terrified, I floored the engine. We circled the neighborhood, screaming.

Disturbing the peace.

Was he hit by a car? Stolen? Hurt? Scared? Helplessness pulsed through our veins. We pulled into the alley behind our house. The sunlight made our congested alleyway, with its tightly placed garages and parking spots, appear almost charming. "No trouble here," it seemed to say. "No, ma'am."

Abandoning the car, we walked up and down the alley, calling for Briggs. "Briggs! Come here, sweet baby. Briggs! Briggs! Briggs?" The hoarseness of my voice mirrored my sorrow.

A shriek shattered my search. Shocked, I turned and looked. It was our neighbor, Whitney. She shouted from her second-floor reading nook, which just happened to lend a clear view of a portion of our otherwise private rear deck. As I looked up, I saw Whitney desperately waving through the open window.

"I saw your dog get taken!"

Chapter 1

THERE IS SOMETHING TO BE said of the human-animal bond — you know that whole man's-best-friend thing. Either you get it or you don't. Dogs have inspired humans to make fools of themselves for years. Whether you are a tough guy who coos sweet nothings to your dog or an owner who switches dog collars based on the day of the week — once an animal has entered into your life, it is impossible to remain untouched. There is something instinctive about this bond: the adoration the animal has for you, the laughter and companionship they bring to your life, and your willingness — and responsibility — to be their protector. That's how it works when you sign on to be a pet owner; above all else, you commit to protecting them.

Josh and I took our roles as new pet owners very seriously. Before we decided to get Briggs, we studied breeds for months. We argued tirelessly about which breed would be best for the space we had, what kind of dog would suit our personalities, and so on. Finally, we settled on a Boston terrier, a good-natured, happy breed that does well in city environments and smaller spaces.

Our three-story townhome on Milwaukee's East Side had virtually no yard, but several parks were just a happy dog walk away. Plus, our small side yard, which was tucked behind a neighborhood church, offered a place where our new pet could take care of business quickly and sniff around freely.

After careful research, we decided we wanted to get our puppy from a reputable breeder who specifically bred for temperament and love of the breed. We weren't interested in a perfect show dog — just a happy, healthy puppy to join our family. Armed with our research, Josh and I visited the breeder in southern Illinois to ensure that it was a tip-top operation.

The drive was six hours each way. Eight of those twelve hours were spent arguing over potential names; one was spent arguing about the speeding ticket I earned; and the rest were spent in happy discussion about how adorable our new puppy was. When we met the litter, we knew immediately that ours was the runt and the oddball of the group. Tiny, with too-big ears, he squeaked adoringly at us and melted our hearts.

Being the responsible (slightly-obsessive) first-time dog owners that we were, we spent the next eight weeks reading books on Boston terriers, investigating training methods, and getting all the necessary components for creating a puppy-proof home.

The day finally arrived when we could pick up our puppy, Briggs. Our drive was significantly shorter this time, as the breeder agreed to drive just north of Chicago to meet us at a rest area where the "exchange" could be made.

A laugh tore from me the second that I set eyes on Briggs. The most recent pictures had made him appear significantly larger.

He was tiny. Tiny in an — I'll-kill-him-if-I-accidentally-step-on-him — sort of way. Immediately in love, we cuddled our new addition to the family. Briggs stared up at us with his warm brown eyes, and stretching up from my arms, he gave both of us a lick.

We'd been approved.

I insisted that we attempt to potty Briggs prior to the ride home. As he ran in circles around Josh, his little body vibrating with joy as he tugged the leash in his puppy teeth, I cried from laughter. This nine pounds of energy was going to give us a run for our money. Ready to begin the journey home, we climbed into the car, Josh cradling our precious new bundle, a bundle that he proceeded to drop between the seat of the car and the door.

Headfirst, that is.

Annnnd, welcome to the family, I thought.

Briggs quickly became the light of our lives, his silly antics pervading our daily emails and text messages. His quirks kept us constantly laughing. From his deep distrust of plastic garbage bags (an environmentalist, perhaps?) to his vicious barking attacks at cooking tongs, he consistently surprised and amused us.

His natural inclination for hilarity revealed itself whenever I attempted to hang up my clothes. Every time a hanger crossed his line of sight, Briggs went through the roof, barking and dancing his way across the room, eyes rolled back in fury. I secretly applauded his stance on putting clothes away. Who really likes to do that anyway?

With an innate sense of humor, Briggs' actions soon had a following among our friends on Facebook. Our research had enlightened us to the fact that Boston's have a sense of humor, but we never expected the immense depth of this personality trait, especially in a dog.

Everywhere we went people were naturally drawn to Briggs. He radiated happiness and loved people. From the dog park to Josh's hurling matches with the Milwaukee Hurling Club (an Irish sport similar to rugby), our dog was a favorite. A wiggly-butt dog, he often laid his ears flat and shimmied his way up to anyone willing to give him attention. Little did we know then that the impact our sweet puppy had on others would benefit him in more ways than we could have ever possibly imagined.

Day 1

A S WHITNEY'S WORDS SHATTERED OUR world, I screamed for Josh. "He was stolen! He was stolen, Josh! Somebody took Briggs!" Whitney's voice fell to background noise as Josh rounded the corner of the garage, panic lacing his steps.

We stared at each other, our reality shifting as Whitney's words fell upon us from the second story like a final, unwanted verdict ruled upon us from on high.

"I saw your dog get taken. I tried to call to Josh, but he took off running. I'm not that mobile, and I wasn't able to reach him," Whitney explained urgently. "I saw...well, there was this man who came between our houses, jumped on the side of the deck, leaned over, grabbed Briggs, and then raced back out toward the alley. I thought it was weird, as nobody ever walks between our houses, but I figured you had friends in the back alley loading the car up.

I didn't realize until I heard Josh yelling a few minutes later that Briggs had truly been stolen."

Whitney went on to describe the dognapper as a dark-skinned male in his early thirties, of stocky build and medium height, and with curly longer hair. She insisted he had some kind of product in his hair because it was shining in the sun. Our neighbor was a credible witness since her thirty years of experience in journalism had trained her to pay attention to details.

Operating on autopilot, I returned to my car. My palms, sweaty and trembling, slipped off the steering wheel as I eased my car into the garage.

There was no longer a need to circle the block.

Knives of pain shot through my lungs as I struggled to breathe. Tears riveted down my face, a cool caress on my flushed cheeks. Josh opened my door and pulled me to him, furiously rubbing my back as I cried into his shoulder.

Briggs was stolen.

Whitney's news changed everything.

Josh took me inside so that we could call the police. I stared blankly at the kitchen wall and immediately felt the eerie silence like a cold weight pressing down on me; the house was too quiet without the pitter-patter of our dog. Josh's words to the police were muffled as images of Briggs flashed through my mind — a half-drunk, manic slide show of what-ifs and could-bes. He was out there somewhere, and I was certain that he was terrified.

Immediately after Josh realized Briggs was missing, we both posted a notice on Facebook — the modern-day version of a "Lost Dog" sign — and asked everyone to keep an eye out for him in our neighborhood. Still reeling from the fact that my intuition had been correct, I achingly updated our Facebook statuses to: "Stolen Dog!"

Stolen Dog. The words stared back at me, their truth undeniable. That would be our battle cry, our cry for help — our refusal to be victims. I began the process of compartmentalizing my feelings. I needed to put my emotions on lockdown, and I needed to do it fast; otherwise, I'd be of no use to Briggs.

My fingers skimmed the keyboard as I frantically posted the information everywhere I could think of, from the Wisconsin Humane Society to the Milwaukee Area Domestic Animal Control Commission (MADACC). I had no idea where to start, but I Googled all animal-related places in the Milwaukee area and posted away. Thinking more deeply, I began to go through my contacts at local media outlets.

"Help. Please help!" Over and over, I sent the plea out.

Our doorbell rang. Instinctively, I turned to tell Briggs to be quiet, but quickly realized my mistake. I watched silently as Josh shook hands with the police officer and assessed him carefully.

Everything from his baby face down to the stammering of his words made it apparent that we'd been sent the rookie. I suppose it was for good reason. In the grand scheme of things, a stolen dog is a minor issue in a city torn by poverty, racial division, a high crime index, and political drama.

Hoping for some advice, I peppered the officer with questions.

"Where can we go? What can we do? Can the police help?"

Officer "Baby Face" politely deflected my questions, took down the little information we could give him, interviewed Whitney, advised me against taking my baseball bat around the city on a search-and-rescue mission for Briggs, then went on his way — and that was that. It was clear that there wouldn't be any police ride-alongs in search of Briggs. Ok, I thought to myself, it looks like this one is on us to solve.

Stunned, and a little uncertain of what to do, Josh and I started bouncing ideas off of each other. Josh's phone interrupted us. Fortunately, it was two of Josh's MHC teammates. They had just seen the Facebook posting and were on their way to help us hang flyers.

Flyers? Of course, I thought. Not everyone is on the Ol' Facebook. We seized that plan of action and raced to the nearest FedEx Kinkos. On the way, Josh and I talked about what we should include on the posters. "Stolen Dog" was a must, as we wanted to evoke an emotional response — emotions being an innate cornerstone of all solid marketing campaigns.

Our first flyer boldly proclaimed "STOLEN DOG" across the top along with two pictures of Briggs. Beneath that, we gave our full address and Whitney's description of the dognapper. We made sure to point out that Briggs' front left paw was white, as if he was wearing a sock.

12

Perhaps putting our exact address on a flyer that was to be distributed citywide was not the smartest idea. Maybe we should have just put an advertisement up that proclaimed how easy we were to steal from — that we were sitting ducks, victims, easy targets. The thought briefly crossed my mind that it was idiotic to put our address on the flyer, but for some reason, my instincts pushed me to leave it.

The rest of the day ticked by — achingly slow — in a fog of posters, tape, and canvassing. There was no plan. No map. No instructions for this situation. Acting solely on impulse and desperation, we stopped, got out, and put up flyers wherever there was room. There was no right or wrong at that point, no protocol. All we could do — and what we had to do — was increase our exposure.

As I walked the eclectic, mostly youthful part of town centered on Brady Street, I came across a group of three men sitting at a table outside of a Jimmy John's restaurant, and I handed them a flyer.

One of the men, a larger black man sporting a brightly colored poncho, read it and stared at me hard.

"Someone stole your dog? That's fucked up."

"Yes, sir. It is indeed fucked up."

Keeping my emotions tamped down, I continued on, handing out flyers to the diners and disrupting happy sub-eating with sorrowful flyers. I also asked if the delivery drivers could put the flyers up in their car windows. We had no idea where Briggs might be spotted, or what a delivered sandwich might lead to.

As I walked out of the sub shop, the three men were huddled over the poster and called me over. It was an oddball group if I'd ever seen one. The large man who'd spoken to me earlier looked at me with compassion. His two companions, a young, thin, white male in a baseball jersey and an older white man with a very long beard and motorcycle boots, studied me intently.

This time, the man with the beard spoke, "You want a free reading?"

"Excuse me?"

"Give me your hand. I'll give you a free reading."

Numbly, I gave him my hand.

He placed a quartz skull gently in my palm and wrapped his gnarled hands around mine, then looked to the sky. Raising his voice, he boomed out, "I can feel your emotions writhing — fear, sadness, despair, and turmoil. I can hear your puppy crying for his mama. He's close, and he can't stop crying for you."

The other two nodded sagely at the man's proclamation.

"Mmmhmm. Mmmhmm. Right on, my man."

The man who'd earlier pronounced the fucked-up-ness of our situation added, "He *is* close, on the 4000 block. Head over there, and you will find your answers."

I thanked them, unsure if I was supposed to bow or give money. Deciding to do neither, I retreated to the haven of Josh's truck and looked at my desperate husband.

"A ragtag group of psychics just informed me that Briggs is sobbing for us and is near. The 4000 block, they said."

Josh stared at me and wrinkled his brow, as if I'd gone insane.

"Psychics? What the...? Do you really want to go there?"

I shrugged. "It's as good a lead as any at this point." Little did I know that it was the first of hundreds of leads. But for now, it was all we had to go on.

Josh agreed. With a deep sigh, he turned the truck that direction. Unsure of what street on the 4000 block to pick, we randomly chose Oakland Avenue and drove there as night settled upon the city and our stolen dog. It was a busy street, and we posted flyers in as many restaurants, bars, and liquor stores as we could. Plodding along, immersed in our grief, we had no way of knowing if we were making any difference. For all we knew, it was too late for Briggs. Kicking this thought from my brain, I insisted we keep flyering.

Little did we know that our efforts that night would lead us to an angel.

Exhausted and having forgone food since the morning, we finally admitted temporary defeat, and stopped for food and drink at our favorite local pizza joint, Zaffiro's. A small restaurant with a comforting, homey ambiance, Zaffiro's has the best slice in town. More importantly, a good friend, Patrick, was tending bar. A dog-lover himself, Patrick had immediately reached out to us to ask how he could help when the news hit Facebook. It was comforting, yet anguishing at the same time to rehash Briggs' story with him while pepperoni-soaked scents assaulted our weary senses. After mechanically chewing, unable to taste the pizza, we sought solace in a beer before heading home for the evening.

Our despair was palpable. We were unable to sleep, yet unable to go on. This time of night would prove to be the worst for us. It was too late to do anything productive, yet we couldn't stop thinking of all the bad things that might be happening to Briggs while the world was sleeping.

Was he taken as "bait" for dog fighting? Why would someone put himself at risk that way in the middle of the day to steal our dog? Images of Briggs trembling flashed through my head. Why did his happen? Do they have a seller lined up? He could be anywhere. The unanswered questions brutalized my brain, making sleep impossible.

Having spoken with MADACC earlier that day, all I could hear was the woman repeating to me, "Ma'am, many dogs aren't pictured on our website because by the time they reach us, they're too injured to be photographed."

Day 2

THE MORNING DAWNED WITH A phone call from a case coordinator.

"I'm sorry, but who are you again?" I asked, annoyance defining my voice. Zero sleep and emotional overload had frayed my already short temper. Her referral to herself as "Case Coordinator" just didn't make sense.

"I'm Kathy, and I work with Lost Dogs of Wisconsin. We help people who've lost their dog and work with them to get their dog returned."

Automatically, I pointed out that Briggs was stolen, not lost. I had to let her know that we weren't bad dog parents. This had happened *to* us; it wasn't our fault.

Kathy, an extremely patient woman, kindly expressed her condolences and spent a half-hour suggesting avenues that we might explore. Speaking with her, I realized that the organization was the real deal and had fantastic resources for people in our position. Bolstered by Kathy's solid suggestions, I hung up, ready to take action.

"Honey, don't miss your oil change appointment," Josh said, cornering me in the kitchen and gently holding me by the shoulders.

Groggy, I stared at him and wanted to scream. An oil change? How can something so insignificant even enter his head at a time like this? Our dog had just been stolen.

"You're 3,000 miles overdue, and we don't know how much driving we will be doing. Maintenance is key. Go." My levelheaded husband ushered me out the door, promising to keep me updated.

But it wasn't his number on the flyers. I'm the one who'd receive any news, I thought as I trudged to my car.

The dealership waiting room was pure torture, like a straight jacket restraining me from action. I watched as the service department huddled over the flyers that I had given them. I hated that their looks of sympathy were for me. I hated that our dog was on the flyer.

After a mental shake to remind myself to remain in lockdown, I opened my laptop to see what I might be able to accomplish while my car was being worked on. Many of my friends suggested that I contact the local news stations, as the loss of Briggs was a heart wrenching enough slice-of-life piece that it might pique their interest. I decided they might be right and composed an email about the story — the subject line burning into my brain — "Our Dog Was Stolen." I called a few stations, and two requested that I send the email over. Shortly after I did so, TMJ4, the local NBC affiliate, returned my call and probed for more information.

"Are you childless? Would you say this dog is *like* a child to you? Did you file a police report?"

"Yes, yes, and yes," I said, wearily.

"We'll be at your house in two hours to film," the reporter said. He shared that they were doing a story about people who treated their animals as if they were their children. Our story about Briggs would apparently be the perfect lead-in for the series.

How lovely for you, I thought, slightly annoyed that our story would help pimp their series. Mentally kicking myself, I forced myself to stop. No matter the reason, this was a huge opportunity to get our story out there. Elated, I rushed home to tell Josh. This was it. This would be what brings Briggs home. Everyone watches the news, right?

Hastily, I did my best to conceal the massive bags under my eyes from a sleepless night of crying while Josh and I waited for the news team to arrive. We kept talking about Briggs, wondering if he'd been fed, if he was running scared, and hoping he was all right, wherever he was. My gut churned with worry, lack of food, and a high-level rage for whoever had done this.

The reporter called to let us know that they were outside, filming the exterior of our house. Nervous, we stepped outside to greet them.

I was unprepared for how painful it would be to see the news truck sitting in front of our house. Similar to an ambulance, news vans rarely signal that a positive event has occurred. News, after all, is mostly governed by the notion that "if it bleeds, it leads."

My hand trembled in Josh's as we waited for the reporter. We are behind-the-scenes people and did not relish being in the spotlight. This was our first major realization that the whole dog-search process was going to drop kick us far from our comfort zone. Steeling my nerves, I pasted a fake smile on my face for the reporter.

The reporter introduced himself, and his cameraman immediately began filming. A little off kilter, I tried to remain calm and appear as the coherent person that I like to think I usually am. I had thought we would have more prep time before the camera rolled — don't they say "action" or something? We took them on a tour of our private deck, through the back alley, and watched as they interviewed Whitney, our neighbor-turned-eyewitness.

When she was finished, it was our turn again. As the microphone turned to us, I did what I could to keep my emotions at bay. I wanted to articulate the facts quickly and drive home the point that we were not going to give up on finding Briggs — no matter what. I wanted to resonate strength and intimidation, not turn into a weepy mess.

The reporter didn't hesitate to go for the emotional questions. "What would you say to Briggs, your darling dog, right now if you could?"

"I love you."

"What would you say to the awful man who stole him?"

"Nothing fit for television."

"How do you feel right now, knowing Briggs is out there and scared?"

"Scared, angry, and sad. How do you think?" And, finally, I administered my plea. "Please keep him safe."

As the reporter wrapped up the interview, he commented about how fabulously the piece would coincide with their news story about people considering pets as family-members.

I nodded. We had a choice: we could either be angry at the media's insensitivity, or we could be thankful for their help. The help and exposure was all that mattered, and I was grateful for the opportunity to take our plight public.

The reporters tromped off with their equipment and Josh left for work, unable to take another personal day. Within moments, I was left alone in the kitchen. My breath shuddered through me as I absorbed the emptiness of the house. Questions assaulted me mercilessly. What do I do? Where do I go? I'm all alone. How do I do this? Is there anywhere I can go on my own, someplace safe?

As these thoughts careened around my head, I stopped and took a deep breath. I knew that sitting at home feeling overwhelmed would not help Briggs.

Right then, I also decided that we needed a mantra.

"Relentless," I said and felt strength flood through me. I can do this. We can do this. If anyone knew how to be stubborn, focused, and difficult, it was me. Now was the time to put all that training to good use.

I wasn't nearly as alone as I thought, as several friends with irregular schedules began to call. Two of our bike-loving friends, Kylie and Blake, rode to our house to pick up flyers; they wanted to post them throughout the city as they rode. I was certain the flyers would make a difference in their hands.

Sadness overwhelmed me when they left. Alone, again, I grabbed a stack of flyers and got in my car, driving aimlessly, as I tried to figure out the best spot to start flyering.

One of my best friends, Kristine, called and asked me to meet her downtown. She had printed flyers and was ready to dedicate her afternoon to Briggs-hunting. Grateful for the support, I swallowed tears. I needed backup.

Downtown, I walked the trendy Third Ward while waiting for Kristine. Almost every shop I went into refused to post my flyer. Dejected, I sat on the curb. Not remembering if I had eaten that day, I felt lightheaded as the sun beat down on me and sweat dampened my neck. I hurt everywhere. My body ached with sadness, and I couldn't help but think about Briggs.

Hearing a horn, I watched as Kristine pulled up. A beautiful brunette in her 30s, she radiates a wonderful mixture of kindness and "don't mess with me," both being traits this mission and I were in dire need of.

Sighing with relief, I let her hug brace me up. It was time to keep moving.

Furious with the Third Ward in general, I insisted that we move further south. Kristine took the reins and drove on, stopping repeatedly at bus stops, empty telephone poles in high traffic areas, and in front of large groups of people on the sidewalks.

My phone rang with an unknown number.

"I saw a dog I'm pretty sure is yours, running alone and headed north. I couldn't get out of my car, as it's a really rough neighborhood. I'm sorry," the caller said, apologizing profusely.

"Let's roll." Without hesitation, Kristine raced toward the neighborhood that the caller had described.

"God, I hate this." I tapped my fingers on the open window while I scanned roads, sidewalks, and alleyways, hoping for a glimpse of black and white fur.

The caller hadn't lied about it being a run-down neighborhood. Every decrepit porch held groups of people, sullenly watching as we drove by slowly. One back yard was filled with people, standing around a grill, drinking cheap beers. The third time we circled, they motioned for each other and reached in their jackets; it was obvious that we were putting people's nerves on edge. It wasn't an area to drive slowly past houses, and they were letting us know that. Unfazed, we continued to circle. If Briggs was there, we had to find him — and quick.

We pulled in front of a small, dilapidated house on the corner, where one man sat on the stoop with his dog. His bare chest gleamed with sweat and dirt, tattoos snaking over his biceps and around his back. He stared us down as we slowed to a stop.

I got out of the car and approached him with a flyer, unsure of the response I would receive. "Excuse me, sir. Our dog was stolen and spotted in this area. Have you seen him?"

He jumped up and moved toward me quickly, his dog right at his side, barking furiously. As he yanked the flyer from my hand, I flinched.

"Those assholes." The man shook his head sadly and took a drag from his cigarette. Angrily, he gestured with the flyer and spat. "Bruno here's been stolen twice. Twice! I recovered him both times, but that shit sickens me. I'll do whatever I can to help."

Relieved, I let out a breath that I wasn't even aware I'd been holding. He gets it, I thought. Dog people just get it.

We picked an alley at random and cruised slowly through. Alleys are not the suggested thoroughfare in that part of the city as they offer very little room for maneuvering, and one can be flanked easily. I shook my head at the ridiculousness of realizing that I was concerned about being flanked in an alleyway. These were not the concerns of last week.

We came to a crawl as we approached a large garage that housed several motorcycles and a variety of burly, tattooed men. This comforted me — these were our people. Milwaukee is home to Harley-Davidson, after all; both of us had many friends and relatives who looked quite similar to the garage inhabitants. The men happily agreed to take flyers and said they'd watch for any sign of Briggs. It was refreshing to have them onboard, especially since they rode the city daily and patrolled their own neighborhood nightly.

As we bumped through gravel lots and nosed behind abandoned warehouses and train tracks, my stomach grew more and more upset. This is such a big city for a little dog. It would be so easy for Briggs to get hurt. The odds were strongly against us. I stared at the train tracks and tried not to cry as I thought about Briggs attempting to cross them. Would he even sense if it was safe to cross? How would he know what to do?

As it grew dark, we were forced to abandon our search, realizing it would serve no purpose to put ourselves in danger. Abandoned warehouses did not feel safe to us. It was time to go.

Driving home, I refused to let my emotions break out of the box I had locked them into. I hated the night for forcing us to stop our search, our efforts shackled by the need for safety.

My phone rang, and I answered it to hear a popular local reporter requesting an update for his evening newscast. In an interesting twist, I had gone to high school with his daughter and mentioned that to him. It's all about who you know, and that tiny, seemingly insignificant connection would get the story run for us four more times that weekend.

Day 3

ATURDAY MORNING SURFACED ACHINGLY
EARLY with the incessant buzzing of my phone.
The news reports had broadened our exposure
significantly. Josh fielded a phone call from his work and
was furious to be called in to supervise. With a kiss and an
apology, he left for work.

Alone. Again.

Anger seemed a productive way to vent my emotions,
and I bitched about Josh's company while I planned my
day. I knew he had to work, and life doesn't stop, even in
the midst of a tragedy.

"Life doesn't stop and start at your convenience, Don-
ny," Walter's infamous comment from *The Big Lebowski*
echoed through my head.

Using Facebook to garner support, I asked people to
meet me at a local pub, The Up and Under, owned by
friends of ours. It is located on busy Brady Street and

would be a perfect meeting place on a sunny day — the street would be crowded. After I arranged a meeting time, I left to print 1,500 flyers and to buy more tape. Perhaps I should buy stock in 3M, the good people responsible for the magic that is Scotch Tape, I mused, as I'd already burned through what felt like hundreds of rolls in a couple days.

On my way to printing, I stopped at the local post office. I hoped the couriers could carry a flyer with them and keep an eye out for Briggs; I desperately needed observant people who walked the streets on my side.

Typical of Saturday, a long line of tense people wound through the post office. I skipped the line of people and asked for the postal workers' help. Sadly, they couldn't — or wouldn't — do much.

As I turned away in frustration, an extremely large black woman in a housedress stepped out of line and blocked my path.

"You were on television last night. I'm so, so sorry to hear about your dog." Her brown eyes radiated kindness.

"Thank you," I said and handed her a flyer, happy that the newscast had made such an impact.

Sighing with sadness, she reached out and embraced me. Pulling my head down on to her gigantic, heaving bosom, she began to pray for me and gently rocked me.

"Please, oh mighty Lord, help this girl find her poor little puppy."

As my face pressed into her sizeable breasts, I was torn between laughing hysterically or burying my face deeper and sobbing. There was something oddly comforting about being cradled by this large, gospel-loving grandmother as she prayed for me. I wanted to curl up and let her rock my fear away. I decided it was best to do neither, so I removed myself from her embrace and thanked her sincerely for her kindness.

And for the prayers. We certainly needed both.

After printing thousands of flyers, all while avoiding the curious gazes of the soccer mom printing school flyers next to me, I parked on Brady Street. What a stunningly perfect day, I thought. The sidewalks were packed with little tables and chairs, pulled out from back rooms and dusted off. Patio weather was finally in full effect. I was excited; the weather was cooperating, and I was sure it would be the perfect day to reach tons of people. I unloaded the car, balancing the boxes precariously as bags of tape swung from my arms. I couldn't wait to get started. I would have a real team today. A taskforce. We'd comb the city and find Briggs. Today was our day.

My phone vibrated with a call from Josh. He was at work, but he couldn't help stealthily hopping on Craigslist now and then to search for anyone trying to buy or sell a Boston terrier. Josh responded to one Craigslist posting and found out it had been placed by a couple who frequented the same dog park where we took Briggs; they didn't know how else to find us and offer help. Apparently, the dog park was up in arms over Briggs' dognapping. God, I love dog people, I thought.

My friend Michelle texted to let me know that she couldn't meet me, but was taping a flyer to her car window since she would be in several areas of the city that day. Noting that as a great idea, I quickly added flyers to my rear passenger door windows.

Hefting the boxes of flyers into my arms, I crossed the street with a bit of a spring in my step. People are helping now. We can do this. We can find Briggs. We *will* find Briggs.

I entered the bar, ready to greet my search-and-rescue team. But as it turned out, "team" in this case meant one person — as in the only person who showed up to help. I stopped. This couldn't be. There had to be more people coming to help. And the one person who had showed up? I barely knew him. He was a guy from a group workout class I participated in, but he loved dogs and wanted to help.

Sadness slammed through me. Why was this so hard? Where was everyone? Of course, I thought. It's the first real day of summer, and nobody wants to spend their time passing out flyers and talking about depressing things like stolen dogs.

Relentless, I reminded myself.

Thankfully, the owners of the bar and another couple, Jocelyn and Chris, arrived shortly thereafter. They all had afternoon plans but were willing to take flyers with them. Jocelyn and Chris would be at Pugfest the next day and planned to hand out hundreds of flyers to the dog owners there as well. Grateful, I handed them flyers and tape.

Unsure of what else I could do, I started making a list of places I'd already been to and tried to think of new ones. Where can I find people who walk or ride the city? We needed bikers, cyclists, runners, and people who are out during the day — pedestrians could be our saviors.

My phone rang, and my friend Caroline told me she was on her way.

Thank God, I thought. I just didn't know if I could do it alone that day, so her call was a huge relief.

Caroline and I started with the closest option — the hundreds of people on patios on Brady Street. As expected, the city was alive with people: people having brunch, people riding bikes, motorcycles cruising, runners doing their exercise thing, and people who were lucky enough to still be walking their own dogs. There was an overall sense of happiness and excitement to the city, as vivid as the sun that had finally decided to shine.

Milwaukee had seen cold weather for too long.

I couldn't begrudge people and their happiness on such a day, but it did strengthen my hatred for the man who had stolen Briggs; he'd stolen that beautiful day from us as well. We should have been celebrating my friend's birthday. We should have been able to relax with a Bloody Mary, our dog at our feet, and laugh with good friends. Instead, I could only wander the streets with my heart torn to shreds and my mind abusing me with unanswered questions. While everyone else was basking in the warmth of the sun, I felt cold and helpless as I fought against a mystery that we didn't know how to solve.

Throughout the day, we stopped at bike shops and motorcycle hangouts and hung flyers on poles in front of places where people were dining on patios. My friend Carrie, an avid dog lover, stopped to pick up some flyers. She lived outside the city and was absolutely distraught about Briggs; she was ready to fight hard to find him. Later, I would learn that Carrie had covered most of her city, a one-woman team.

"Our dog was stolen...our dog was stolen...our dog was stolen," I repeated over and over again. After a while, the words lost their meaning, as if it was some mindless saying I was reciting, a fake repetition of something that couldn't possibly have happened. It felt like we were telling someone else's story.

I learned then that it's entirely possible to move from feeling numb to feeling frozen. As I watched people's distraught reactions and recounted the story over and over, I learned to cut to the most important details and to keep my emotions out of it.

After a long day of work, Josh came to pick me up, and we made the decision to head to the north side of Milwaukee — no-man's land. Unlike other bad areas of the city, this area was an absolute wasteland.

We drove the streets and looked for light poles and bus stops where we could hang our flyers. As we stared at the surrounding landscape, our tension grew. This place was empty and utterly soulless.

The late afternoon sun cast a warm glow across the abandoned, concrete jungle, but even the sun's radiance couldn't pierce the cold heart of that neighborhood. I almost couldn't stomach the thought of Briggs being in this place.

Not here, I prayed.

Josh skidded to a quick stop at every pole and bus stop.

"Hurry," he said, his eyes urgently tracking the rearview mirrors.

I had my flyers taped and ready and moved as fast as I could, but I could feel eyes on me, watching. Still, I never saw anyone. What does that say about a neighborhood? I wondered. The first beautiful day of summer, and nobody is outside. There were no dogs, no flowers, no children.

A few abandoned parking lots held groups of men, huddled around cars. As we drove past, they straightened, staring us down. Their unspoken message was clear: *You aren't welcome here.*

My fear for Briggs outweighed their message.

As the light grew faint, we abandoned our mission. Driving home, we stopped to flyer another high-traffic street. My friend Carrie had mentioned she would try to cover that area while she was babysitting her niece, Cleona, that day. My eyes glazed with tears as I saw hundreds of flyers covering trashcans, bus stops, and poles. Carrie had come through.

Day 4

ANOTHER DAY DAWNED, STILL WITH no word
on Briggs. I laid in bed, listening to Josh's quiet
breathing next to me. Rolling over, I stared at
Briggs' empty bed, and my chest constricted, tight bands
of fear crawling up my back. It was hard to breathe, and
anxiety threatened to engulf me. The oppressiveness
blanketed me as heavily as the humidity that had taken
hold of our city overnight — thunderstorms were in the
forecast.

Will the tape give way under the rain, banishing our flyers to the gutters with the rest of the litter? The thought
almost brought me to tears. My working knowledge of the
strength of tape had stopped at grade school construction
projects, but I was rather certain that tape and water didn't
play well together.

Josh's first hurling match was later that day, and I noticed him weighing the pros and cons of going.

I looked at him in disbelief.

"Don't tell me you're even considering going off to play some intramural game when we should be out hunting for Briggs." Furious, I stomped away from him.

I felt the anger building, but I wasn't really mad at Josh. I knew he was harboring an incredible amount of guilt and sadness because Briggs' abduction had happened on his watch. I suppose I just needed a target for my anger. We are often hardest on those closest to us, and I didn't mean for Josh to take the brunt of my frustration and heartache. Nevertheless, as my anger reached a boiling point, I was prepared to rattle off every last reason as to why Josh shouldn't go to his game. I was ready for a fight.

Calmly, Josh explained to me that his team might not have enough players and would have to forfeit, but he offered to call his captain and find out. Feeling childish, I stormed around the house, making angry noises. I was frustrated because we weren't moving. We weren't doing anything. We always have to be doing something. How else could we save Briggs?

Josh came back from his phone call with the "all clear" from his team captain, saving me from a poor display of temper. He looked at me questioningly.

"Now what?"

I was the queen of this search, yet I had no strategic plan. We would come to realize that this was one of the hardest parts of the search. Where have we been? Where have our friends been? How do we coordinate efforts?

Will we overlap? What makes the most sense? What's the best use of our time?

Time. How much time does Briggs have? Torturing myself with thoughts of Briggs' death, I again forced my emotions back down.

We decided to go after the animal lovers first. Because it was Sunday, we were sure we'd find a few at dog parks and pet stores. Unfortunately, there's really no rhyme or reason to where these places are located. Trying to map a path that made sense would take hours. The inefficiency was enough to make me want to scream.

Reasoning that dog parks made the most sense, we started there. The hot wind kicked up dust and ripped flyers from our hands as we spoke with dozens of concerned dog owners. Lack of sleep and the humidity slowed our efforts. A storm was approaching.

Moving on, we mapped out the best route to several pet stores. Some welcomed us with open arms and were prepared to offer all the help they could; others, quite unexpectedly, hustled us off of their property like we were trying to sell them life insurance. I simply could not believe that any pet store would refuse to help. Wasn't their very business to support animal lovers? Refusing to accept no for an answer and sticking with our "relentless" mantra, we learned to simply smile nicely, walk outside, and hand flyers directly to their customers as they parked. "No" was not an acceptable answer for us.

Later that day, we communed with Josh's MHC friends, Clodagh and Brian, a young couple in their early thirties. Clo and Brian were the early responders when our cry for help had first gone out about Briggs. In need of sustenance and a bit of a break, we met them at a local pub.

We sat at the bar and ordered our food. Listless, I picked at the cracked corner of a menu and let the noises of the bar settle around my shoulders. Bacon-wrapped scents enticed my empty stomach as I nursed a cold cider, hoping the alcohol would numb me further. I was seated at the far end of the group and had tuned everybody out when I felt the wind shift through the open doorway, accompanied by a sudden temperature drop.

The storm had arrived.

The sky began to weep; I tried hard not to do the same. I stared down blindly at my food, my appetite gone. All I could see were hundreds of flyers getting washed away, and defeat weighed on my shoulders.

My phone rang from a restricted number. I gulped and answered it, hating callers that intentionally hid their phone numbers.

"Yeah, yeah, yeah. So…I've got your dog. What's the reward? I got him," a male voice boomed at me.

Stuttering, I tried to think of the right things to say.

"Um…uh…can you, um…tell me what he looks like?" I asked.

"Yeah. He black and white and have a bent leg."

"A bent leg?" I asked, confused. What the…?

"Yeah, his front leg, the one with the sock. It's bent. You offerin' a reward. What is it? I want the reward."

It was then that I realized he was simply describing the picture of Briggs that we had placed on the flyer; his leg was bent in the picture. My core went cold.

"Great," I said. "If you'll send me a picture, we can meet and exchange the reward for our dog." I hung up and saw everyone staring at me, their mouths agape; they were shocked at my callous disregard for the caller.

"What the hell, Tricia?" Josh asked, furious, and obviously thinking I'd screwed everything up.

I explained that the caller just wanted the reward.

"He described the *picture* of Briggs to a T, yet he couldn't give me any real information."

My phone rang again, and I quickly handed it to Josh. He thinks this is so easy — let him handle it this time, I thought.

I watched as Josh fumbled through the call and hung up. He looked at me in understanding.

This was another glaring problem in our plan: We had no script, no right way to handle those kinds of calls. All we could do was try to keep the person talking and go on instinct. We had no idea where our lead would come from.

As the last traces of the storm moved out over Lake Michigan, we left to assess the damage. We followed Lincoln Memorial Drive home and tried to place flyers in the main intersections. The tape struggled to stay on the wet poles, only to give up the fight against the water.

We'd hit our limit for the day, and I refused to break down over tape. It was time to go home.

As night fell, I waited for my parents to come over to collect their cat, which we'd been watching while they'd been vacationing in Mexico. There's something about seeing your parents in the middle of a tragedy. Part of me wanted to hug my mom and cry for hours, but the other part felt compelled to reassure them that we were okay and could handle it.

I could see how upset they were and how helpless they felt. My dad was ready to wage war on everyone and encouraged us to move outside of Milwaukee. My mom was more concerned about our welfare and wanted to make sure we'd been eating and getting enough sleep.

Grateful for their concern, but beyond exhausted, we hugged them and sent them and their cat, Scrapper, on their way. Thank goodness Scrapper's safe, I thought. I'm not sure if I could have lived with someone else's animal getting stolen on our watch.

After they left, we sat on the couch in our silent house, drapes drawn, and looked at each other. When the phone rang again, I stared at it, nerves making me punchy. Taking a deep breath, I answered.

"Hello? Hello? I'm calling about your dog!"

Bar noise filled my ears, music, glasses clinking, and people laughing. I could hear people yelling to the caller — laughing and shouting about Boston terriers. As the caller stumbled through her story of buying a Boston terrier for $100 ("No, say '$200'!" someone shouted in the background), my stomach turned. I tried to get details about where she was and what the dog looked like.

"Its tail is docked," she said.

That stopped me. Briggs' docked tail wasn't visible in the photos. All of the sudden, I was very, very scared for Briggs. I tried to convince her to meet me and suggested we meet by a police station. The click of a disconnected call doubled as her answer.

Shit, I thought. Shit, Shit, Shit.

"What are you doing, Tricia? You can't ask them to meet you at a police station. Nobody's going to do that!" Josh said, his frustration obvious.

"I can't help it, Josh! I don't know what to do! It is almost eleven p.m. on a Sunday. I don't know what to say or how to handle this. Tell me a safe meeting place. I mean, how do I know it's not a setup? Maybe they're plotting to jump us because they know we'll have a cash reward on us," I said, frantic.

The woman's words harassed my mind: "His tail is docked."

Ten minutes later, the phone rang again. Silently, I handed it to Josh, but as soon as the caller heard a man's voice, they hung up. We reviewed the details of the phone call and Googled it, only to find they'd called from a bar in the heart of the city. Distraught and unsure what to do, Josh and I reviewed our options.

Three minutes later, the phone rang again. Frustrated, I grabbed it and answered.

"Hello!"

"Hi. You don't know me, but I have a Boston terrier, too, and your story has me really upset." The caller pro-

39

ceeded to break down into choking sobs and talked my ear off for a half-hour about how upset she was — all at nearly midnight on a Sunday.

I gently disengaged from the phone call. How can we keep doing this? I wondered. We hadn't realized that we would have to manage other people's emotions. Why was I talking someone through hysterical sobs when we were the ones with the stolen dog? Why was I reassuring her? The irony of it floored me. My strength was reserved for Briggs, and Briggs alone.

Day 5

HIS TAIL IS DOCKED."

The phrase haunted my dreams throughout the night. Operating on little sleep was quickly becoming the norm. I suppose the worst part of any tragedy is the expectation for victims to carry on as normal when nothing feels normal anymore. Normal would have been Briggs' pink-tongued kisses serving as my alarm clock.

As a marketing consultant, I have a variable work schedule. Some days I am required to be onsite, but I often work at home, setting my own hours. Monday was typically a work-from-home day, so I decided to tackle a few of the promotions I needed to do for a client. Working with furious energy, I quickly finished my projects for the day.

Family and friends agreed to call local vets and shelters for me. Kylie, Kristy (an old high school friend), and my mom checked in repeatedly throughout the day as they contacted more places for us. It was nice to have a phone team.

Reasoning that the perpetrator had to be working or living in the area, I decided to tackle the streets surrounding our neighborhood. Sunshine mocked me as I walked down the sidewalk with an arsenal of flyers in hand.

Walking silently and observing the neighborhood, I ran through the possibilities in my head. How could something like this happen? Briggs must have been stolen by chance because there really would have been no way to plan it, I reasoned. There were simply too many variables. I didn't work a set schedule and often worked from home throughout the week. Josh worked second shift and was in and out during the day. Briggs was rarely on the deck, especially during the week, and our deck was private, not viewable from the street or alleyway. We did not have any sort of nine-to-five routine, nor did we let our dog out on any semblance of a schedule.

So how could anyone plan to steal him? How long had we been watched? Was it simply a spur of the moment decision? I was sure somebody had to have seen Briggs at some point and just decided they wanted him. Just how long the man staked us out, though, was undetermined. Then again, it could have all been left to chance. What if someone simply walked between the houses, saw Briggs, and grabbed him? But then they couldn't have had a car waiting in the alley. Perhaps they circled briefly, after seeing Briggs? As my thoughts staggered around my tired brain, I reached no conclusion.

My phone vibrated in my pocket, and a concerned citizen was on the other end.

"Well, gosh, I hate to bring this up — I really do — but have you considered the fact that he might be being used as bait for dog-fighting? Again, I *reeeaallly* hate to bring this up, but you should be aware that this happens," she said, secretly delighting in the drama.

Quietly, I thanked her for her assistance and hung up, though what I really wanted to say was, "Really, random person? Really? Has it occurred to you that maybe it has already occurred to us, and that perhaps we don't enjoy constantly being reminded that our dog might be having his neck torn out as we speak? Unless you can lead us to an actual dog-fighting ring and/or have a useful tip that will help our search, could you please just shut up? Thanks."

Blinking back tears, I mechanically returned to taping up posters, though now with my mind fixated on the image of Briggs, bleeding, teeth pulled, and trying to defend himself in a corner. I hated these dramatic people that called to tell me about such scenarios, offering us no help at all. They delighted in the twisted drama of presenting us with ever-worse possibilities, the way everyone dramatically whispers about someone who dies in a horrific manner. It was human nature at its finest, and it was getting on my nerves.

My phone vibrated again, and I reluctantly answered it. The caller introduced herself as Megan and offered to stop by to pick up flyers. And then there's the other side of the coin, I thought.

I also immediately felt uncomfortable. It wasn't that I didn't want people to help us, but I had no idea who to trust — particularly when I was offering a reward. I had no idea if callers really wanted to help, or if they were just waiting to catch me with the reward in my pocket. I had quickly grown sick of feeling unsafe.

Megan agreed to meet me at a busy street corner to pick up the flyers. She pulled up in a nondescript Nissan and immediately approached me with her arms open in a hug. Megan began talking about how sorry she was and told me all the places she'd be willing to put up flyers. Happy to have the help, I gave her a stack of flyers, we exchanged numbers, and we continued on our separate ways.

Megan would proceed to stop by every day for more flyers — *every day*. You can't buy that type of goodness, I realized, and she single-handedly restored my faith in those that were willing to step up and help.

Day 6

CARS FLASHED BY IN A blur. A rock hit me in the face, its sting minor compared to the terror that gripped me. I screamed as I glimpsed a flash of Briggs, running. He was too far from me. He couldn't hear me.

"No, no, no," I sobbed. I jolted awake from a nightmare of Briggs trying to cross the highway. Josh held me as I gulped air, trying to quiet my mind. Even sleep wouldn't let me escape. I dragged my tired body out of bed, my stomach still churning from an anxiety-filled night of disjointed dreams.

Rage overwhelmed me, and I couldn't seem to stop it from growing. I had to leave the house for work that day, and I was mad that it would take me away from the search for Briggs. Briggs was all that was important to me at that moment, but I couldn't call in or quit. Resigning myself, I started the drive into work — trying not to think about my panic-laced drive from the week before.

Keeping my eyes on the road, I answered my vibrating cell phone. It was Josh.

"I've been looking at that psychic website you sent. I think we should do it."

Surprised, I asked him if he was sure. My fairly level-headed husband humored me when it came to my interest in astrology and tarot card readers, but like most men, he wasn't exactly into it. Earlier in the week, I had presented Josh with an animal communicator website I had learned about. A friend had found a pet psychic pamphlet at a pet store and suggested it. The communicator was known for specializing in missing pet cases.

"I feel like this will give us hope or at least an action plan for an area of the city we can focus on. It's worth a shot — I'll pay the $250." Josh said. He knew I needed something to keep me going.

I agreed to contact the psychic later that day, though I wasn't certain if I believed in the power of psychics. As a true skeptic, however, I was always willing to try something and base my opinion on experience. As far as I was concerned, we had nothing to lose.

Mulling it over, I begrudgingly climbed the steps to the drab brown building that housed my company. The beige hallway with equally beige carpet and wallpaper were a perfect representation of my feelings.

Even though I wasn't a fan of the company (or its office decor), I worked with some great people there. As soon as I set foot inside, the women immediately converged upon me.

"How can we help? What can we do? We are so sorry!" A few of the men stopped by my desk, too, dog lovers who were willing to help. The manager sent out an office-wide email containing the "Stolen Dog" poster.

I sat at my desk, in a valiant attempt to focus on work-related topics. The overall beigeness of my office and the fluorescent lights began to press down on me in my suffocatingly small cubicle.

My cell phone proceeded to ring…and ring…and ring, forcing me away from work.

"How much is the reward?"

"I think I know where your dog is, but I want to know about the reward."

"Give me the reward first, and then I'll tell you what I know about your dog, lady."

"I need money."

"I'll kill your fucking dog if you don't pay up!"

Astounded, I simply hung up on the last caller. People did not care about my dog. All they cared about was lining their pockets. Money — the ultimate motivator.

We had been cautioned by the Lost Dogs of Wisconsin group not to release the amount of the reward because some would use it as a starting point to open negotiations — like a ransom for our stolen pet. It hurt my heart, knowing that I'd probably have to deal with someone like that. When did our society get to the point where being a good person was contingent upon a monetary reward?

Overwhelmed by the amount of nasty phone calls, I decided to go ahead with Josh's suggestion and contact the pet psychic. Perusing his website, I realized he was located in Georgia. Hmm, I thought, I wonder if that will affect the, um, clarity of his reading? I had no idea how such powers worked. What if it's a rainy day? Will that cloud his vision?

Laughing at myself a bit, I emailed the psychic. He quickly responded to my inquiry, but unfortunately, he was working with his own animal, hoping to help the dying cat to "transition." He said he wouldn't be able to help us for a few days.

I sent him the information he asked for, but I was I worried about his mental state. Will he even be able to help us after his animal's death? I hoped that the emotional drain wouldn't affect him, and that he could remain professional.

Thanking him again, I returned to my email to see forty-three messages waiting in my inbox. In under an hour, my email had filled with notes from concerned friends, family, and updates from Matt, my tech geek friend from college who'd appointed himself my unofficial "Briggs" social media campaign manager. I scanned Matt's email and acknowledged his insistence that I create a Facebook page for the Briggs' campaign; we needed a central location that we could direct people toward.

I thought it over and came up with a name that would immediately grab readers' attention and inform them of what we were about. Thus, the "Stolen Dog—Bring Briggs Home" Facebook page was launched that very same day.

My good friend Marisa designed a background headline graphic to showcase Briggs' white sock and sent it to me to serve as the header for the page. That image would eventually be shared by hundreds upon thousands of people.

I clicked "publish," sat back, and prayed.

"Please, please, please," I said.

Day 7

I BLINKED AWAKE. MY VIBRATING phone had fallen off of my bedside table, dragging a notepad with it. I blurrily weeded through my full voicemail box, trying to determine if there were any actual leads among the messages. My bullshit radar was working overtime these days.

One voicemail was from an elderly woman who was now terrified to leave her house after seeing our flyer. I called her to reassure her that it was all right to go grocery shopping; her tinny voice crackled at me through the phone, her relief apparent.

On the drive into work, images of Briggs flashed like a sordid pinwheel through my mind. Is he being taken care of? Is he even alive? Should we be making our search so public, or will we scare this man into going underground with him? I pushed those uneasy thoughts aside and tried to calmly run possibilities through my head, making mental notes of avenues that we had yet to explore.

I stomped down the beige hallway into work, boiling with hate over the ugliness of the carpet, only to fall lower still as everyone's faces fell when they heard that Briggs had not yet been found. Yeah, I feel the same way, I thought.

Channeling my rage into the productive action of hating the office's I-Think-I-Run-The-World-Sales guy, I gave him a mental middle finger as I passed his office.

My day was filled with blindly answering calls, attempting to get work done, and trying to hold my head up in the fluorescent prison that was my cubicle. Josh checked in with me constantly, sharing every idea he and his co-workers could come up with.

I came to realize that this was another difficult part of the process. Everyone had an opinion, and while people thought they were being helpful by offering suggestions, I was getting hundreds of suggestions a day. The compound effect left me feeling like a failure — as though I wasn't trying hard enough.

After an interminable day of work, I spent the remaining daylight hours placing flyers in transitional neighborhoods by myself. Josh's phone call from earlier that day played through my head. He'd been hanging posters in some difficult areas by himself before work and had left me with explicit orders to avoid certain neighborhoods when I was out on my own.

"Don't you dare go into a bad area without me," he said.

"What if I get a call and you aren't here?" I asked.

"Call Paulie or Chuck," Josh said, referring me to two of his friends who could protect me — in other words who were licensed to carry.

As the shadows deepened, I abandoned my flyering. Going home, I beat myself up some more, this time for not always being able to do it all on my own. Whenever I had to stop and go home, it felt like I was giving up on Briggs, trading his safety for my own.

Nighttime is the worst, I thought. I noticed how empty the house felt without Briggs, especially while Josh was at work — often until midnight or later. It's amazing how quickly our perception, our illusion, of safety shifts when we become victims.

Our home is a three-story lofted townhome. My office is on the third floor, and there's only one staircase down to the first floor. As I sat at my desk, I felt like a sitting duck for anyone who had a flyer with our address on it — all those people out there who now knew I was sitting on a reward.

I was in a constant state of fear and anxiety. Our address was on over 2,000 flyers throughout the city, I was on the bitter end of receiving threatening phone calls, and there was no dog to bark an alarm. I attempted to shake it off and tried to focus on my role as Campaign Manager of Operation Bring Briggs Home. The Facebook page was growing steadily, and our community offered consistent support. As I was following up with the comments and messages from the amazing community of followers, my phone rang.

"Call restricted," my phone display blinked. I tensed. Restricted numbers meant the caller had something to hide.

"Hello?" I answered nervously.

"Yeah, uh, is this the Boston terrier person?"

"Yes. Hello."

"I killed your muthafucking dog, bitch! Dead mother-fucking dog," the man's voice shouted hysterically through the phone, followed with maniacal laughter.

I couldn't help picturing Briggs with a broken neck, lay-ing on a concrete floor, muddy and bloody, his cold body tossed away. My vivid imagination was quickly becoming my worst enemy. Refusing to give a reaction, I quietly hung up. I was shocked by the evil in this world. Another part of me wasn't surprised in the least. With our increased exposure, we were targets for all the drunks, freaks, schemers, and scum that Milwaukee had to offer. And like any city, Milwaukee's got plenty of each.

One thing that I do know is that while I don't always have time to help others, I'd certainly never go out of my way to make it worse for someone in need. These callers sickened me.

I tried to control my breathing and willed the fear back. Refusing to stumble or be dissuaded and demanding that I remain relentless, I worked through the night until Josh came home.

Day 8

S ILENCE WOKE ME. I PUZZLED over this until I realized I was listening for Briggs to do his wake-up "ear flap." He always did a funny thing: he would shake his ears out, causing a distinct flapping sound that would nudge me out of sleep, and I'd peer over the bedside to see him waiting for permission to come up for morning snuggles. As soon as I left for work, he'd take my body-warmed spot in the bed and cuddle next to Josh. I stared at his empty dog bed, covered in his favorite blue sleeping bag. I had loved that sleeping bag for camping trips, but Briggs loved it more.

My phone beeped with a text message: "Hey, you don't know me but I handle the Twitter account for La Perla (a local Mexican restaurant). I saw your Briggs poster and would like to send out information if you're okay with that. We have 10,000 followers."

Exuberantly, I performed a fist pump that would have made the cast of *Jersey Shore* proud.

"Thank you so much!" I texted back.

He responded and introduced himself as Steve Schumacher, then promised to tweet the information later in the afternoon. Calls like that always managed to wipe out the cold fear that the scarier calls left. A tweet isn't much more than a minute of someone's time, just 140 characters — yet it meant everything to us. The community support guided our perseverance and demanded that this was not to be our fate.

That's the thing about battles. If you stop leading the charge, everyone will just go home.

In a far better mood, I headed off to work at the beige dungeon. On the drive there, I remembered something even more encouraging: Today was psychic day! Elated, I called Josh to remind him.

"Okay, baby," he said in a cautionary voice, "but just be prepared for whatever he tells us."

"I know, I know," I said.

On the psychic's website, several disclaimers were posted that we would receive an immediate phone call if our animal had "transitioned." *If Briggs is dead,* is what they meant. Hoping that no news was, in fact, good news in this case, I tried to push that grim thought aside. I rushed to hole up in my fluorescently lit, dull cubicle, bypassing the office gossips. Hoping not to be distracted, I tried to concentrate as questions flooded my mind. Should I call the psychic? Does he need more information? Was the email I had sent enough? When will he begin the map dowsing? What if it's going on right now? And what the hell is map dowsing?

With my hand anxiously beating out a *tap-tap-tap* staccato rhythm on the desk, I refreshed my email constantly. This is it, I thought. This is how it works in the movies, right? Missing kids, missing dogs, missing keys, whatever: the sad couple's last-ditch hope is to contact the psychic who leads them to the answer. We're going straight to the source. Yes, this psychic will know the answer. He has to.

Tap-tap-tap-tap.

I grew more anxious with every minute that passed. I had to attend a sales meeting at three, and I didn't want to be away from my computer or my phone. Not today, I thought. I can't deal with this today.

Then, just like that, the little envelope blinked in my screen. I had incoming email, and it was — *hallelujah* — from the psychic. He didn't call. He emailed me. Briggs was still alive.

Briggs was alive.

Breathless, I read the email. The psychic wanted to know if I knew anything about one particular neighborhood, one he was getting a strong sense about, and he said he'd give me more details shortly. Trying to stay calm, I shakingly stacked my notes for the sales meeting and snuck a quick text to Josh to update him. Debating for a moment, I slipped my phone into my folder. It would be joining me for this particular meeting.

I made my way to my seat in the conference room and sat quietly, waiting for the meeting to commence. My phone continued to vibrate against my leg, hidden from sight beneath the table.

We launched into a discussion about a direct mail campaign. The aforementioned, egotistical sales guy continued to overrule my marketing idea with his ingenious slogan idea: "Perhaps our service is a better fit." I was floored that the vice president would even agree to such a 1980s, backwards campaign. Refusing to be talked over, I expressed my displeasure with that particular direct mail campaign, prompting the sales guy into an attack.

"That's just because you don't want to work hard, Tricia."

My already raw emotions boiled over.

"Excuse me? You think I don't want to work hard? You don't even know the definition of hard work, of how to truly hustle. You sit there making one phone call an hour, then walk around the office looking for snacks. You've closed one sale since you've worked here — ONE! You have no concept of what hard work even means."

Furious and my voice shaking, I couldn't help but smile. It felt good to stand up to someone who spent his days putting others down.

Silence fell, and everyone in the room stared at me in shock. I stared right back at my adversary, refusing to back down, and then glanced around at the others.

"Are we finished here?"

The sales guy refused to make eye contact with me and stormed out of the conference room, slamming the door on the way out. Damn, that felt good, I thought, and quickly retreated to my office to check my phone and email.

Finally - the psychic had returned our email with a detailed account:

> **Hi Tricia,**
>
> **I had an opportunity to communicate with Briggs. Here is what he shared with me:**
>
> **He said he has been staying inside mostly and is well.**
>
> **He said he gets moved around a lot and visits a different place during the day.**
>
> **He showed me an older Latino woman (50's/60's) that he visits during the day.**
>
> **He showed me two small elementary-aged children and a Latino man that he visits during the night.**
>
> **Both locations are close together and appear to be apartment buildings.**
>
> **He gave me the sounds of air brakes from a truck or bus.**
>
> **He showed me a small park that he has visited.**
>
> **He showed me a brown brick church or building near the park.**

He showed me a dark (grey, silver, black) older car that he has been in.
He said he rode in a car for a long time when he was taken.

I then pulled a map of the area and performed detailed map dowsing. Below is the area that holds the greatest energy signature at this time. I have placed push pins in areas that may match what he has shared.

I would suggest visiting the buildings marked first and any close by that are similar. Talk to the building managers to see if they have seen him or know of anyone who has a new dog/puppy. See if they will post signs and send an e-mail message to the residents.

Visit the park areas and speak to the grounds crew to see if they have seen him and will post in the area. See if they have a website or Facebook page where information can be posted.

Visit the bus stops and speak to the drivers. See if they have seen him or heard anyone speaking about a new dog/puppy. Check with the churches, schools and preschools in the area to see if they have seen him and can post on their website and Facebook accounts.

Stay in close contact with the breed specifics and other rescues and shelters in this area. They may look to sale him, and if they can't quickly, they may give up and turn him in. Check Craig's List and other local free publications to see if he is posted. Also, any known postings or locations where they sell dogs (non-pet stores). He has not said he has been with other dogs or has been attempted to be sold.

Check the local restaurants, grocers and convenient stores in your neighborhood. The man may work in the area or visit those locations.

Check with neighbors and businesses to see if they have hired any people or companies to do repairs or yard work to their homes or buildings.

I have asked Briggs to show himself often and allow people to assist him. I let him know that you are looking for him, love and miss him very much. It is very important to stay positive and visualize his return to you.

My entire body went warm, and my heart soared. Briggs was alive.

Ecstatic, I forwarded the email to Josh and then stared at the map. It was a Google picture map, and I could see the true image and color of the buildings. The psychic had placed arrows next to the spots that best resembled the descriptions Briggs had given him, as well as where he sensed a strong energy from Briggs. I knew the neighborhood, and it was located only about fifteen minutes west of where we lived. It was the kind of neighborhood we drove around, not through.

I was stuck on the description of an old woman caring for Briggs during the day. Is this a grandmother to the children he stays with at night? Is she kind? Briggs had so much energy, and I couldn't imagine his needs could possibly be met by an older woman. Where is he sleeping? How do they take him outside? Did they put a new collar on our dog?

I thought about the children the psychic had mentioned. Children were a wildcard, in my opinion. Normally, I would have felt comfortable with Briggs playing with kids, as they have the high-level energy necessary to entertain a Boston terrier. However, after receiving a few heinous prank calls from children and hearing their laughter over the idea of killing our dog, I no longer felt that way.

I tried to focus on the best-case scenario. My hope was that Briggs had been stolen by a dad who worked in our neighborhood, had seen Briggs, and had thought Briggs would make the perfect gift for his children. At the very least, that would mean he was being taken care of. On some level, whether we ever got Briggs back or not, that was the very best I could hope for — that he'd been taken by someone who would love him and treat him well.

I answered a phone call from Josh as I left work with my map in hand and ready to begin my reconnaissance mission.

"Tricia, promise me you won't go into that neighborhood without me," my husband implored.

"Dammit, Josh. You've got to be kidding me." Busted, I slammed my hand on the steering wheel.

"Don't do this," he pleaded. "I can't be constantly worried for your safety. Just wait one more day. We'll go tomorrow, together. I promise."

Josh, as usual, was the one with his head properly screwed on.

Reluctantly, I agreed. Yet — Josh had only told me not to go "into" the neighborhood; he hadn't said anything about going around it. Maybe if I just skirted the surrounding, busier streets. Who knows? Maybe Briggs would be outside for an after-work walk.

Megan, the girl who'd been showing up daily for stacks of flyers, called to find out what the psychic had discovered. I told her about the less-than-desirable neighborhood, but warned her not to go alone, the same warning Josh had given me. Briggs was our dog so putting myself at risk to rescue him was one thing, but I couldn't knowingly lead or allow others to head into danger. She promised not to go; all the while, I was driving directly towards the area myself, blatantly ignoring Josh's orders and certainly not practicing what I was preaching to the woman on the other end of the phone.

As I was making my way to exactly where I had promised not to go, Megan called again. Panic laced her voice as she admitted that she'd directly ignored my warnings and had driven through the neighborhood.

"Um, okay. So you were right. I definitely should not have gone there alone."

She went on to describe that the streets were very narrow in the heart of that neighborhood; on a nice, summer day, people milling on the streets could easily converge on cars, and it wouldn't take much for drivers to find themselves stopped, with a gun pressed up against the window. She promised to heed my advice the next time I told her to avoid certain areas, and then disconnected.

Marveling over the pure heart of this stranger, I hoped all of our hard work would ultimately pay off for us. Oh wait, didn't somebody just say something about me not knowing what it means to work hard, I thought, shaking my head.

Needing reinforcements, I called my friend Paulie. He agreed to join us the next day and serve as our driver as we headed deep into the inner city. He offered to call a buddy of his who used to live in that area and he said he'd get the word out and would drive through the neighborhood before dusk that evening. Relieved, I picked another neighborhood to plaster with flyers and waited to hear back from Paulie. Fortunately, the wait wasn't long.

"Don't go into that neighborhood alone, Tricia," he said, echoing Josh's warning and Megan's report. He went on to explain that the nice weather had drawn everyone out to the streets. He also informed me that his old friend had gotten back to him; he'd moved out of that neighborhood when a dispute between his two cousins ended in murder — a dispute over a mere $400.

"It isn't worth risking your safety, Tricia, so you have to wait on Josh and me. We'll go tomorrow, around ten a.m., when people are sleeping or at work."

Knowing when to pull back, I agreed.

Sitting at home that evening, I contemplated everything the psychic had said. I put the good energy out there and talked to Briggs, letting him know we were coming for him. I talked to spirit guides, God, or any spiritual messenger who might carry my words to Briggs.

"Please keep him safe and tell him we're coming for him."

The vibrating of my phone interrupted my prayers and supplications. My phone buzzed and beeped excitedly — signaling multiple text messages, emails, and Facebook alerts. I glanced at my computer and saw that emails had poured in; Briggs' Facebook page had exploded.

"Whoa…what the…what's going on?" I wondered.

The first text message was from Steve at La Perla.

"You're blowing up! All the restaurants and news stations are sharing you on Twitter!"

Witnessing social media at its finest, I sat there, astounded, as Briggs' story went viral.

Apparently, while I had been talking to psychics and dealing with work issues, restaurants all over Wisconsin had tweeted about it and offered to chip in to bulk up the reward. Bars, stores, bloggers, and all the major news stations were catching wind of it and spreading the word. Local DJs wrote about Briggs on their blog and sent friend requests to me left and right on Facebook. I logged on to the Facebook page for Briggs and thanked as many people as I possibly could, but it was close to impossible to track how many people had shared it.

That night, Briggs' "Stolen Dog" poster was shared over and over and over, reaching far beyond our neighborhood. The energy was in the air; I could feel it, and I hoped Briggs could too. I hoped he knew how hard everyone was looking for him.

Then, as if some Big Bang had taken place in all of cyberspace, all of my alerts sounded. Phone calls, texts, emails, and Facebook posts and messages flooded in all at once. Astounded, I stared at my computer screen: Rose McGowan, a famous actress and part of the WB's *Charmed* cast, had tweeted the Briggs' poster.

And just like that, we'd gone national.

Day 9

WE HAD LAUGHED FREELY THE night before, a much-needed respite from our recent, humorless routine. Josh had come home with a smile on his face for the first time in over a week. We celebrated with pizza and a beer, and almost giddy, we clinked "cheers" over the attention we were garnering. Briggs wasn't home yet, but in less than nine days, we'd made a serious impact.

It felt good to know that we could make a difference, and every little success gave us a reprieve. We realized that others were helping, that others cared, and that we did not have to be so hard on ourselves.

With a new sense of purpose, we geared up for our search and rescue operation. It was time to delve deeper into the crime-ridden neighborhood that the psychic had told us about. This was a part of the search that I would not be discussing with my parents.

I thought about what I would wear that day. Josh thought I was nuts — but I knew I was right on. I put on skinny jeans, a tight black tank top, and simple sandals. I left my dark hair curly and put in some big hoop earrings. I knew I would draw some attention, but figured I would blend in for the most part.

We drove halfway to the neighborhood and walked the streets, posting flyers everywhere while we waited for our friend Paulie to pick us up. When I taped a poster up in front of a laundromat, I heard a whistle and looked over my shoulder.

A man slowed his Lincoln and gazed out the window.

"Damn, girl!" He said, looking me up and down. I gave him a nod and continued taping. Secretly, I was pleased. Things would run more smoothly if I blended in.

Josh was furious.

"You're getting the wrong type of attention! What is wrong with you?"

Paulie pulled up right then, allowing me to ignore Josh's question.

As soon as I was situated in the back seat, I informed my husband and Paulie of the plan.

"Here's the deal. You two will stay in the car. I want you to tape posters ahead of time, pull up at the corners, and I will be the one to get out. I know you don't like this Josh, but the attention I'm getting is flattering. Nobody is trying to start anything with me. You two, on the other hand, are going to attract the wrong type of attention. Only get out if you think I'm in real trouble. I can handle it otherwise."

Unhappy with my plan, they had no choice but to agree. They knew I was right, and they couldn't argue with the truth of it. Girls are simply less threatening than men; all things considered, a few shout-outs would be a whole lot better than negative attention ending up in an unnecessary confrontation.

As we began our cruise of the streets the psychic had marked on the map, my sadness increased. The area was so desolate and angry; I could almost taste the unhappiness around me. Bedraggled apartment buildings clustered around sunken houses, trash littering the yards.

We pulled up at each intersection that had a light pole. Inevitably, I would get shouts or questions from people as I taped up flyers. Stopping in front of a school, an attitude-laced shout startled me from my taping. I looked on as a hysterical, extremely large woman shouted at a group of men in a parking lot. I couldn't help but smirk a bit — she was the epitome of a strong woman with an attitude who wouldn't take shit from anyone.

When she saw me watching her, she turned her wrath on me.

"What you looking at, you dumb bitch?"

I ignored her and continued taping.

"Hey. You. Dumb bitch. You can't fucking hear?"

I glanced over my shoulder and saw the group of men laughing as she raged at me from across the street. The car lingered silently behind me, waiting. I quickly hopped in and watched through the back window as the woman hurled a piece of trash at us. The men laughed as her arsenal fell short, and she directed her anger back at them.

Classy, I thought.

We decided to stop at a main intersection, one with bus stops on every corner. Paulie and Josh joined me. We split up with signs and hit the bus stops, speaking with everyone who was willing to talk to us.

After we got back in the car, I consulted the map.

"Time to move in deeper," I said. I knew we'd be heading into the tough spot where roads narrowed, streets were quiet, and people turned a blind eye to trouble. Bad things happened quickly there.

As we drove deeper into the city, I spotted what looked like a major corner. Since there were several poles for flyers there, I asked Paulie to stop. I got out and looked around, my skin crawling. It was almost certain that I was being watched. I put up flyers on each corner and hurried back to the car.

As I made my way to the safety of Paulie's vehicle, a Suburban peeled around the corner and blocked my path. I stopped and gasped as I realized another car was hovering on the other side — just like that: I was flanked.

Does this kind of stuff really happen? You have got to be kidding me, I thought. Did I trip some kind of wire that let them know strangers were onsite? Word traveled fast apparently.

The driver of the green Suburban was a young man with dreadlocks. He leaned out of the window and motioned me over. I kept an eye on the other car; ready to sprint around the back of the Suburban if I heard any car doors opening. I prayed that Josh and Paulie would stay right where they were, in case I had to make a run for it.

Shit, shit, shit, was all I could think. I knew that even if I could make it to Paulie's car, he would have a hard time getting his car between the Suburban and the other car.

The driver of the Suburban looked me up and down.

"What's on the flyers, yo?"

"Our dog was stolen," I said, staring him down.

"No shit? Let me see one of those," he said, holding out his hand.

I reluctantly walked over and handed him a flyer through the open window. I tried to look past the Suburban to see what was happening with my guys. I knew they couldn't see me.

Meanwhile, the driver started asking me questions about Briggs. As usual, he wanted to know the reward amount.

We had already decided not to post the amount on the flyer, but if anyone asked us in person, we would say the amount. In all honesty, we knew we couldn't go into these neighborhoods and promise thousands of dollars for the return of a dog; if we weren't outright ignored, we would be laughed at. People here had long ago stopped believing in promises. That thought had prompted us to settle on a moderate, believable amount.

"If you find our dog, it's $500, no questions asked."

"No shit? All right. I'm on it. Can I call you if I have questions?" the young man asked.

"Of course," I replied. I thanked him and gingerly moved away from his car, praying that it wasn't a stupid move to turn my back on him. I climbed into the back seat of Paulie's car and exhaled with relief.

"What did he want?" Josh asked. Both he and Paulie were more than a little panicked. Both hated to be caught in I-don't-know-what-to-do situations, and it had been hard for them to watch what was going on.

"He was actually really nice," I said. "He just wanted to know what the flyers were about and what the situation is."

As if on cue, my phone rang. Green Suburban guy asked a few more detailed questions and agreed to contact me later if he heard anything from "his peeps."

"Let's go to the spot with the most arrows on the map," I said, directing Paulie to the heart of the neighborhood.

Paulie pulled his car to the side of the street by a parking lot that was adjacent to a school and a church. This was it. This was the prime location that the psychic had marked. Across from the parking lot was a row of houses with run-down porches. Almost all of the porches had at least one person sitting on them, watching our every move.

I got out and made my way over to the first pole at the entrance of the parking lot. Nervous, I hitched the flyers closer to my chest. My neck tingled from being watched. I wanted to position the poster to face the traffic, so that drivers would see it on their way into and out of the parking lot. With the hope that the church or school was attended by the Latino family mentioned by the psychic, I posted flyers everywhere. The thought of this all being a wild-goose chase spawned by a two-bit psychic trickled through my mind. I had no idea what to believe.

My back was turned to the parking lot. As I worked away at a particularly stubborn and annoying piece of tape, I was startled to see the car door slam, and Josh run across the parking lot. I whipped around just in time to see a tough-looking guy running in my direction. Josh bolted past me, intercepting and stopping the guy. Words were exchanged, thankfully, not fists or bullets.

Tense, I looked at the car. Paulie nodded at me, letting me know he was ready. Suddenly grateful for Wisconsin's Conceal and Carry law, I waited.

Josh and his "friend" walked to a van parked close by, finished their discussion, and Josh turned and walked quickly back toward me.

"Okay?" I silently mouthed at him.

He nodded.

"What was that about?" I asked, not particularly fond of guys who hung out in their vans in parking lots.

"Well, I saw him running at you. He just came out of nowhere. I didn't even think. I just jumped out and intercepted him. He claimed that he just wanted to see the poster, and he backpedaled a lot. I didn't want to go to his van, but he said his brother raises dogs and might know something about Briggs. I gave them flyers, and the brother just went on and on about his dogs, then said he'd help us look. I really don't like this, Tricia. It's a dangerous area, and I don't like leaving you vulnerable outside the car," Josh said. "I stopped the guy this time, but who knows what else could happen?"

"I know. I know," I said. And just in case he was having thoughts of ending the search for today, I insisted that we keep flyering.

As we finished putting up flyers on that block, I made myself look at every porch-sitter, right in the eye. One man glared at me long and hard; I pointed at him and then at the poster, and he spat on the ground. I knew then that all those flyers would be torn down by the next day. It didn't matter. We'd made our presence known. Round one was over, and we'd be back for more.

Later that night, the calls began:

"I'm gonna kill you, you dumb bitch."

"I'm gonna rape you."

"I found your dog and killed it, bitch."

"Fuck you and your dumbass dog."

Sitting alone on the third floor of our house, I cradled my mace in my palm and hung up on every caller.

Day 10

OUR FIRST THREE-DAY WEEKEND OF the year, Memorial Day weekend, began with a wave of sadness that blanketed both of us in a miserable haze. Who are we kidding? I thought. A three-day weekend is a time for travel and cookouts. Surely no one's going to give up their grill-outs and baseball games to help us hang flyers. Still hopeful that we might get some support, I texted a few of our friends for help.

The brakes on my car were in dire need of replacement, and Josh selected that day, of all days, to change them. I looked at him in disbelief. Why can't he stop trying to fix things and focus on what needs to be done to get Briggs home? Looking back, I realize it was Josh's way of coping with sadness; he couldn't find Briggs for me, so he was trying to fix whatever he could. It was hard for me to see it at the time. It was far easier for me to pick a fight with him.

Pissed off, I drove Josh's truck to the store. I'd been doing some research on posters and had a new idea about how we might attract more attention. I purchased all the supplies we'd need and drove home to set up our creative studio. Josh's co-workers were on their way to help with the brakes, but in the meantime, we churned out the new poster design.

We simply taped our original "Stolen Dog" posters to larger, hot pink and neon orange poster board. Using reflective tape, we doctored the posters to catch the light. We added huge block letters proclaiming, "REWARD!" and "STOLEN DOG!" across the top. We would place those larger signs at main intersections, and we were sure they'd garner attention because they were simply too big and bright to be overlooked.

We also decided to translate flyers in Spanish and proceeded to stuff hundreds of envelopes with them. They would be easy to drop into mailboxes of veterinarians' offices and other businesses across the city.

Our friends Clodagh and Brian texted us back and agreed to meet us at our house with their conversion van. Clodagh, originally from Ireland, owned an Irish shop in Elm Grove and often traveled to set up at various fairs and festivals. Their conversion van, used to store goods while she traveled, offered enough room for several people and dogs.

My friend Marisa also called and offered to join us along with her two Great Danes, Lemmy and Lulu. I was ecstatic about our human and canine street team for the day. Neon posters and giant dogs would draw a huge amount of attention to our cause. In a stroke of what I considered to be luck, my brakes could not be changed due to a missing tire key; suddenly, I had more helpers on hand to aid in the search. Taking our pile of Spanish flyers, Josh and his co-workers left to head for the South Side of the city. With a quick kiss, he advised me to stay safe, and I said the same to him.

Shortly thereafter, Marisa showed up with her beautiful Great Danes. The gentle giants loped around our house, looking for Briggs; they could smell that another dog lived there. As I told my friends about the prior day and the horrific phone calls that we'd been receiving, Lemmy and Lulu skidded to a halt near me. As if sensing my sadness, they pressed against my legs. I was happy to have those friendly, massive protectors by our side that day.

Clodagh, being a properly feisty Irish woman, insisted that we head right back to the area where we'd been the day before.

"Why not make your presence known again, but this time with two huge dogs?"

I agreed with this reasoning, and her husband Brian was all for it. I wanted to make sure Marisa was comfortable with taking her dogs into that area, and she felt it was fine. In her experience, she'd learned that most people were frightened of Great Danes simply because of their size.

Grabbing our large, hot pink flyers, with the dogs at our side, I felt strong. There would be no mistaking our message today.

It was another sunny day, the perfect weather for Memorial Day weekend. I imagined what we normally would be doing: heading to friends' barbecues, taking Briggs up to my parents' lake home so he could play in the water, and trying to get the first tan (or in Josh's case, sunburn) of the year. Instead, we were pulling up to an empty parking lot next to a street basketball court full of people who were betting on the teams.

As we parked, I noticed through the side window that the basketball game had stopped. A conversion van full of strangers slowly pulling into an empty lot in this neighborhood was as expected, the kind of thing that caused a stir. As we unloaded the dogs from the car, we heard murmurs from the court. A few small children started yelling. The Great Danes were already doing their job.

We decided it would be best to divide and conquer. Marisa and I took Lemmy, while Clodagh and Brian took Lulu, and we aimed to hit every pole on both sides of the street.

The basketball court grew even quieter as we walked past. One man crossed to the other side of the street, and children shouted questions at us. Sullen stares greeted us from the players; they didn't like us being there, but they were too afraid to say anything because of the dogs.

When I reached the site from the day before where I'd pointed at the man on the porch, I saw that the flyers had been ripped down. I looked across the street. The same man was sitting on the porch, glaring at me. I looked at him again, and he looked at me. I looked down at Lemmy, back at the man, and then taped up a huge poster over the place where the remnants of the last one were.

This time, the man gave me a nod.

We walked for hours that day, and anyone who saw us hurried to cross the street to avoid the dogs. We waited outside of busy places like Walgreen's and gas stations, handing out flyers to shoppers as they tried to back away from Lemmy and Lulu. By the end of the day, we'd met our goal. We had clearly made our presence known in the neighborhood that the psychic had identified. We could only hope that the Great Danes, the neon posters, and the locals' word-of-mouth would reach whoever had Briggs. We wanted him to feel the pressure was building, that we were willing to do whatever it took to get him, and that we were closing in on his home turf.

Eventually, we decided to go to the South Side to rendezvous with Josh. It was the Hispanic side of town, so we took our Spanish flyers with us. We continued our walk with the dogs, hanging flyers and passing them out to anyone who would take them.

The streets were busier on the South Side, teeming with life. It was a vivid community, filled with happiness. Children played outside, flowers adorned the windows, and festive music filled the air. It didn't feel as angry and ominous as the neighborhood we'd just come from.

The Great Danes did their thing, stopping traffic, drawing attention, and generally creating a disturbance.

One man walked out of a store and jumped back in mock horror: "Daaaaamn! We used to Chihuahuas down here!"

We all laughed. A much needed relief.

When we arrived home that night, we were too antsy to sleep, so it was decided that whiskey and a fire on the back deck was in order. As Josh built the fire, I rummaged in our junk drawer for a paper and pen. Carrying these outside, I sat down next to Josh. We sipped our drinks and contemplated the flames.

"Do you think he's ok?" Josh asked.

"He has to be. He just has to be."

Nodding, Josh stared into the fire.

"Let's send up our thoughts." Brandishing the paper, I told Josh to write what his thoughts were for Briggs.

Staring down at the paper, my eyes blurred as I wrote: *Please, help us. Keep him safe. Help us, we need help.*

As I tossed my hopes into the fire, I prayed to any and every spirit warrior I could, asking for help, asking that they would send us a sign; praying that they would give us something, *anything* to keep us going.

Little did I know our sign would appear the very next day.

Day 11

THE NOW FAMILIAR, BUT STILL unwelcome, silence woke me.

As I gazed down at Briggs' empty bed, I couldn't help thinking of him. Where is he? Is he safe? I wonder if he's scared. Is he too hot? Do the people who have him know he likes to burrow under blankets to sleep? Is he with other dogs? Do they know he has trouble breathing in humidity and can't exercise too much when it's hot?

I thought about what the psychic said and hoped that the grandmother who might be caring for him during the day recognized his sweet soul and was treating him gently.

I tried not to let my mind wander where it shouldn't, but I kept seeing flashes of Briggs running across a street or having to defend himself. I reminded myself of all the times at the dog park when Briggs had stood up for himself when his Frisbee was stolen. He had a very strong defensive instinct that could get him into trouble in the wrong situation. I prayed that he would use it if he needed to, but mostly, I just prayed that he was not in any situation that would require it.

I tried to focus on action steps. Each day, I picked the problem back up and twisted it, looking at it from a new angle. What could we do to make a difference? What hadn't we tried yet?

When Josh woke up, we discussed our options for the day. We'd spent the past two days covering the area that the psychic suggested, so we decided to consider the other information he'd given us as well as the eyewitness description that our neighbor had given us. All things considered, we felt that we could safely assume a Hispanic man had stolen our dog. With our freshly-translated Spanish flyers, I was excited to paper the Hispanic neighborhoods more thoroughly.

Josh and I discussed what we knew of the Hispanic cultures. Knowing of their deep faith tradition, we decided to head back to the South Side and put flyers up as church services exited. As we drove, Josh and I talked about our city and its diversity.

"I hate that we have to make assumptions based on the race of the person who stole our dog," Josh said, his hand beating out a familiar staccato rhythm on the steering wheel.

"I know, I know. I hate that we have to base our search off of an eyewitness description and a psychic, but it's all we have to go on."

When we arrived on the South Side, we saw several food trucks setting up and smelled the delicious aroma of peppers and onions frying. Luckily, I had the forethought to translate a few sentences into Spanish.

"Buscando mi perrito!" I said, excited to use my Spanish on one food truck driver.

After my haphazard attempt to explain our situation in Spanglish, he happily agreed to tape the poster to the side of the truck. It was an excellent way to increase our exposure since hundreds of people visited the trucks daily.

Josh and I circled the South Side, putting flyers up at grocery stores and in front of churches. We quickly realized that food markets were prime real estate for us; without fail, huge groups of people congregated around the bulletin boards at the exits. As we looked more closely at the bulletin boards, we realized that the community interest was for the multiple job postings. I knew that any Briggs flyers posted there would be seen.

After we finished our loop of the South Side, Josh and I headed west. He was determined to go to Gander Mountain that day to purchase a handgun that I would feel comfortable handling. It had been a running argument in our household. Though I much preferred my mace and baseball bat for protection, it appeared that Josh didn't feel as confident in my weapons of choice. I had to agree. My concept of safety had been severely shattered the day Briggs was stolen, and a Louisville slugger no longer seemed like it was going to cut it.

On the drive, I brought up a sensitive subject.

"I can't believe that strangers are busting their asses to help us," I said.

"I know!" Josh replied.

"I'm surprised that some of our friends who live around here haven't really reached out that much to help," I said.

"I know. It's…disappointing," Josh acknowledged, putting it lightly.

Perhaps it's the times of tragedy that shine the brightest lights on friendships. Josh and I were not so naïve as to think everyone valued animals and pets as highly as we did. To some people, a dog is just a dog — a replaceable pet. To us, Briggs was something more — he was family — but we couldn't force others to take action. We were simply surprised that some friends didn't realize just how much we were hurting, and fewer than we expected offered the support that we needed. We certainly didn't expect everyone to drop everything that they were doing and make our problem theirs, but reaching out and asking how they could help or simply asking if we were okay would have meant a lot to us.

My friend Meghan emailed, texted, and called daily, even though she lived in Colorado. Her entire office was following the story and offering suggestions. She did this naturally, without thinking, and in the best way she could from across the country. We couldn't help but wonder why people we barely knew or didn't know at all were capable of reaching out when some of our friends were unable to do so. The Briggs situation was proving to be more life changing than we had ever anticipated, in ways we probably would've preferred to remain ignorant of.

Switching subjects, Josh perked up and began lecturing me on gun safety. Trying to listen, I despondently picked at a rip in my jeans. This was not what I wanted to do with my day. Resigning myself to time not spent hunting for Briggs, I headed with Josh into Gander Mountain.

As the cool air of the store washed over me, I examined the hundreds of guns lining the wall.

"Yippee," I muttered to myself.

Josh, on the other hand, was already off and running, like a kid in a candy store. As a lifelong hunter, he quickly found his happy place amongst the artillery and ammunition. As he held up model after model of gun to me, I just looked at him blankly; showing me gun styles was the rough equivalent of me asking him which shoes I should wear with a maxi-dress.

We settled on a gun that he felt I could comfortably fire, purchased ammunition, and left the store. With the mandatory wait period, Josh wouldn't be able to pick it up for a few days.

It was early afternoon, and we were already exhausted. Heading home, I thought about what else we could accomplish on a Sunday evening on Memorial Day weekend. We couldn't come up with much, but the world had other plans.

After a refreshing shower, I walked downstairs and found Josh texting in the kitchen.

"What's up?" I asked.

"I was thinking about going out to meet Chuck for drinks," Josh said.

Flabbergasted, I stared at him.

"Excuse me?"

"What? We aren't doing anything more for the night."

I was instantly enraged. How could he even think of leaving me right now? My phone rings every two seconds. Sure, most of it is just prank-callers, lunatics, perverts, and liars, but what happens if we get the call — the one we have to make a move on? What if I need help? What if someone finds Briggs? This wasn't the time to split up. I needed my partner, my protector, by my side.

I said as much and not in a very nice way. My diplomatic skills had reached their limit some time ago.

As the argument heightened, the doorbell rang. Immediately tense, Josh grabbed his knife. I peered through the peephole and saw a couple in their late forties, standing at our door with a child. I opened the door.

And the angel spoke.

Day 11: Evening, Part I

TO SOME, ANGELS ARE A joke. Signs, spirits, positive energy, and the greater "meaning" is little more than nonsense. My personal belief system falls somewhere between Catholic and a general belief in spirituality. A confirmed Catholic, I rarely attend church and long ago found that I did not entirely believe in the religion. What I do believe in is the power of faith, prayer, God, and spirit energy. I believe that people have spirit guides and that their loved ones remain near after they pass on. I found — and find — this comforting.

When it comes to spiritual belief, people will follow their own personal views. Nobody will know the truth until they cross the threshold between life and death. In the interim, faith steps in. I believe that the energy we put out there to accomplish the things we want and asking for help or guidance from spirits (the universe, God, or whatever deity one prays to) is natural and has its place in human history for good reason.

The night before, Josh and I had sent up our individual prayers in the fire to ask for guidance, a sign, something to help us to keep going. Sheer determination and perseverance can make dreams happen, but it never hurts to ask for a little help along the way.

Our sign arrived in the form of the couple at our doorstep, more specifically, a woman named Annmarie. Casually dressed in a light jacket, she was an attractive woman, slight in build, with beautiful eyes that dominated her face. She looked deeply into my eyes when she met me, as if she was reading my soul. Later, I would learn that she was, at least in her own way. I instantly felt a connection with her but was at a loss to explain why.

"Hi. I'm Annmarie This is my husband Kirk, and our son Wyatt."

"Hello," Josh and I both greeted them, crowded together in the door.

We didn't invite them in.

"I saw your flyer and just had to come talk to you. I know it seems odd to just show up at your doorstep, but I need to talk to you." Annmarie went on to explain that she had seen our flyer at the 4000 block of Oakland Avenue while they were eating dinner, and she absolutely could not get it out of her head. On the way home, she'd forced Kirk to return to the restaurant so that she could copy our address and contact information down.

The 4000 block was where we had been instructed to go that very first day by the ragtag group of psychics outside of the sub shop. They had told us that help would be found there.

As Annmarie rushed to explain how she could help, it took a while for her words to register. It turned out that she was the Vice President of a media group that managed five radio stations, and her husband owned Hal's Harley-Davidson, a predominant motorcycle business in town. She asked me to write down her email address and to send her more information; she'd help however she could.

I hugged her and thanked her for her help. Then, stepping back inside, I looked down at the paper in my hand, the one with her various email addresses on it. My hand couldn't stop shaking. I just stared at her name on the paper and her email. Why is this one person, of the hundreds of people who've offered to help, resonating with me so much?

It was a simple exchange of words — an encounter that lasted under five minutes — yet it pierced me to the core.

Josh looked at me.

"Wow. That was really nice of them."

"I have to email her right now." I rushed upstairs and proceeded to send Annmarie a detailed email about everything we'd done for Briggs, as well as all the information we had about how and when he was stolen from us. Rejuvenated, I raved to Josh about all the potential opportunities we now had. This was a woman with clout. Who knows the type of exposure she could offer us? All I knew was that she would help.

Our sign had arrived.

Day 11: Evening, Part II

WHEN THE PHONE RANG LATER that evening, I excitedly reached for it, certain it was my new best friend, Annmarie, ready to take over Milwaukee with the Briggs campaign.

"Hey, are you the owner of that dog who got lost? That black and white one? 'Cause the neighborhood kids seen him, and I think I know where he is," a young girl's voice squeaked at me through the phone.

My heart skipped a beat.

"Josh!"

Josh ran upstairs and paced as I delivered the details in a rapid rush of words.

The caller's name was Anna. She was a young girl in a group home and was calling from the same rough neighborhood where the psychic had sent us to look for Briggs. The neighborhood kids were out running around and told her they'd seen our dog, the one from the poster.

"Tony the Junkyard Man has him," Anna casually informed me.

"Who is Tony the Junkyard Man?" I asked, images of a masked man with a meat cleaver and rabid dogs flashing through my head.

"Everybody calls Tony that 'cause he collects everything in sight. The neighborhood kids seen he got this dog and asked him where he got him from, and he said a guy sold the dog to him."

"Can you tell me anything about the guy who sold the dog?" I asked.

"Yeah, my uncle cuts his hair. He got a fade last week, but nobody's seen him around since then. He's Puerto Rican," Anna said.

"Hmm. Puerto Rican, you say?"

"Mm-hmm."

"And you say nobody knows where he is?"

"Right. Ain't nobody seen him since he sold the dog to the Junkyard Man."

"Okay, Anna. Can you do me a favor? Can you go to Tony the Junkyard Man's house and see if the dog is still there? Is there a way you can sneak and take a picture?" I asked, tension lacing my words.

"Sure. I'll call you back after some kids go check it out."

"Remember that there's a reward, no questions—"

She hung up before I could finish, but I was glad to see she hadn't called from a restricted number.

Josh's breath came out in tiny puffs as he stomped around the third floor.

"This feels right. This is good."

I filled him in and bounced around the room, trying to contain my frenetic energy. I couldn't help getting a little dig in.

"See? This is why I didn't want you to go out without me."

With a well-deserved eye-roll, Josh resumed his pacing, and I realized it probably wasn't the time for I-told-you-so's.

"I don't understand. Who is this Junkyard Man?" Josh asked.

"I have no idea. Anna said she's sending the neighborhood kids over to check the situation out. If it is Briggs, how do we go in and get him? We can't just barge in there making demands. That'd be like asking for trouble, especially at night."

As we silently contemplated how to handle the new situation, my phone rang again.

"Hi, Anna. What did you learn?" I asked.

"Well, the kids went over there, but Tony wouldn't let them in. He left and locked the door and told them to keep out, but they said they can hear a dog barking, and they know it's a black and white dog."

"Can someone go talk to Tony and find out how he got the dog? Let him know that we are offering a reward?"

"We can try."

"Anna, do you know Tony's address?"

Anna rattled it off to me, and I couldn't believe it. It was right in the middle of the neighborhood the psychic had led us to. A Hispanic man had sold a black and white dog to someone else and hadn't been seen since the transaction. We were sure that Tony the Junkyard Man was our man, and we were convinced Briggs was in there.

"Okay. Thanks, Anna. We really appreciate your help. I don't want to bring the police in or anything. I just want to know if it is our dog." I hung up the phone, but didn't know what to do next.

Josh looked at me and asked, "Should we go over there?"

We thought about it and realized again that it was Sunday night of Memorial Day weekend. People would be out partying, barbecuing, and likely not sober. Cruising through a rough neighborhood and stopping at Tony the Junkyard Man's house to insist that he show us a dog that he bought (fair and square as far as he knew) might not exactly qualify as wise. That much we knew.

I hated the predicament we were in. It was so tiring feeling like victims, like we had no control over our situation. We constantly felt like our hands were tied. As risky as I knew it would be, I ached with wanting to go over there immediately.

Luckily, Anna called us back.

"The kids came back," she said. "Tony doesn't want a reward. He says he wants to keep the dog, and he won't let us in the house."

"Okay, Anna. Thanks for your help. We may stop by or have an officer stop by. Please, please, please tell Tony that he is not in trouble. Nobody is in trouble. We don't care about anything other than our dog's safety."

"Okay. My phone is dying, and curfew is coming up. Let me give you a friend's number, just in case," Anna said, shyly.

"Anna, where do you live?" I asked.

"Um, in a group home. They have some rules about phones and times."

"All right. Thank you, Anna. You did the right thing by calling us, and we really, really appreciate you reaching out and trying to help. Not everyone has been so helpful." As I hung up, I looked at Josh. "Let's go."

"Nice try, but we're calling the cops in on this," Josh said, staring me down.

Regardless of his insistence to involve the authorities, I had a strong suspicion that if he had received the call when I wasn't home, he would have already been knocking on the Junkyard Man's door.

"Oh, sure. I can't go just because I'm a girl, huh?"

"I've already lost one thing I love, and I'm certainly not going to let another stand in harm's way. I can't protect you all the time, but I can now."

It appeared that we had hit the proverbial rock and hard place, but I conceded, and we called the cops. We were concerned that this would ruin our reputation on the streets, but saw no other immediate option. The Junkyard

Man would move the dog quickly if he knew he was in trouble.

We sat on the front stoop to wait for the cops. Since it was a holiday weekend, we imagined it would be a while, and we were right. Forty-five minutes later, they showed up. Standing on the sidewalk in front of our house, we detailed the calls from Anna.

The cops were skeptical and seemed a bit perturbed to be out on a missing canine call. They asked a lot of questions and hemmed and hawed, making me angry. Finally, I told them I would go to Tony's house, with or without them. Realizing that I was serious, they quickly instructed us to stay put and said they'd go check it out.

We sat on our stoop for what felt like forever, barely talking. The smoky aroma of grilled meats teased our nostrils as cheerful noises from backyard barbecues drifted towards us. Our street was happy, and I was jealous. I wanted that freedom — that carefree attitude. I wanted us to be with Briggs, at a barbecue, with other dogs for him to run around with.

I idly wondered what Tony the Junkyard Man's house was like. From the way he yelled at the kids who'd asked about our dog, I imagined it was utter filth. His neighborhood title didn't exactly lend itself to high expectations for good hygiene or a healthy home environment.

"What if it isn't Briggs?" Josh asked me.

"Then we get up tomorrow and keep looking," I said, having no other answer. All I felt was an icy pit of absolute certainty burning in my stomach. We had to keep going forward; there would be no stopping or giving up.

Still, I felt like our window of opportunity was closing. What if all of this pressure we're putting on everyone actually ends up harming Briggs? Are we scaring his captors into killing him or dumping him alongside the road? Are we making the right decisions, doing the right things for Briggs' sake? All I could do was trust my instincts. I knew we had to keep going, even if that meant I'd eventually be the last one standing.

"Are you worried that we're sending the wrong message by sending the cops in?" Josh asked.

"Yes. We've saturated the neighborhood with flyers and posters, telling people to call us, and the first time we have a real lead, we send in the police. The last thing we need is for people to think the police are going to show up every time they call about possibly seeing Briggs."

"I know. I was thinking that too," Josh said, realizing the error of our ways. His broad shoulders were tense and he continued to twist his hands anxiously.

I just wanted to throw something.

"At the very least, we made a point of asking the cops to be extremely nice and to tell Tony that there is a reward, no questions asked." But I knew it wouldn't hold much weight on streets where cops were the enemy.

As time stretched on, we once again fell silent. Left to our own thoughts, I wondered if this was the answer to our fire prayers from the night before. Or was it the woman who showed up at the door, offering to help us with her connections? Wouldn't it be wonderful if Anna's tip put an end to all of this?

Headlights sliced through my musings, and the police car slowed to a stop in front of our house. Nervous, we ran to the car as the officers got out.

"Is it him? Is it him?"

I already knew the answer; I could tell by their demeanor. They were both wearing that face cops wear when they have bad news.

"I'm sorry, but that man doesn't have your dog. We took a picture just to make sure."

One of the officers held up his cell phone for me to peer at the tiny screen. There, a black and white Border Collie looked forlornly back at me. He had a white blaze down his forehead, similar to Briggs' markings. My shoulders slumped. Hope slipped from me as I thanked the officers.

"That's it. We're going out," Josh declared.

Numbly, I agreed. I couldn't sit at home and obsess over all the awful things that might be happening to Briggs. My grasp on my emotions was tenuous at best. Anna's story had checked all the boxes. Letting go of it nearly defeated me. We both needed to blow off a little steam before we imploded.

The city lights twinkled at us as we trudged along the sidewalk to meet up with our friends. Patio tables fought for sidewalk space, and lines spilled from restaurants as people waited to see and be seen. It was hard for us to be out. Harder than we had realized it would be. A fog of

sadness cloaked us, making conversation stilted and difficult. People either wanted to hear every detail of what we'd
been doing to find Briggs, or they tried to quickly change
the subject to trivial matters that meant nothing to us. We
had become the "Debbie Downer" couple. Soon, a subtle
space grew around us as people drifted away to find light-
hearted conversations. Serious conversations were for another time.

The night took mercy on us and came to an end. Our
friends went home to sleep in and gear up for Memorial
Day festivities. Our silent, dark house waited for us, a veri-
table tomb of sadness and loss. As we walked inside,
Briggs' absence was louder than his presence had ever
been. Briggs used to greet us in a very unique way. We only had to hold our hands above his head and open and
close them three times, then say, "I love you." Each and
every time, he barked three times, which was his way of
repeating those words back to us. I held out my hand to
the empty living room.

"I love you," I silently mouthed as I opened and closed
my hand three times.

Day 12

A SLOW THROB OF PAIN signaled it was morning. A dull headache from one too many cocktails mixed with the grating pit of sadness in my stomach. The day off seemed to ridicule us. There are no days off when your dog's missing. The tedium screamed at me. Constricted by our inability to stop, I ignored invitations to Memorial Day barbecues and focused instead on how to use our open day.

The air seemed heavy with more than just impending storms as I logged onto my email to filter through hundreds of suggestions. An email from Annmarie, the woman who'd shown up on our doorstep, jumped out at me.

She started by saying that she never emailed from home because work kept her so busy that she demanded her home life be left alone. Her email went on to say that she couldn't stop thinking about us and had already composed a list of ways she might be able to help. For starters, she'd reach out to her radio friends and ask to have a few of the morning radio hosts get our story on air. We couldn't have bought that type of coverage — or if we could have, it would have been far beyond the reaches of our budget. Grateful for the help and hope, I replied to Annmarie with an overabundance of thanks.

Reenergized, we decided to continue with our Memorial Day plans. Our friends, Clodagh and Brian, had offered to take us out in their van again, this time including their own pit bulls as part of our street team. First, Clodagh had to run a fundraiser for the local Humane Society at her Irish shop in downtown Elm Grove, during the local Memorial Day parade.

Desolate, we plodded our way toward the entertainment. As we picked our way through the crowds of revelers, the heat pressed down on us. A bubble of sadness surrounded me as a kaleidoscope of parade images bounced past. The colors were too bright, the people too happy, and all I could feel was emptiness.

We reached the store and greeted Clodagh. Her infectious energy and love for animals radiated through her as she told us about her fundraiser for the Elmbrook Humane Society. Reviving our spirits, Clodagh introduced us to the shelter dog she had at the store that day to help promote the fundraiser.

I laughed at the shaggy pup and missed Briggs deeply. The puppy seemed to sense my sadness as he exuberantly licked my face.

As we waited for the Memorial Day festivities to die down, we outlined our plan. Fearless Clodagh was determined to go to the worst parts of the city. Through her animal activism, she was well aware of the places where dogs were treated the worst and knew it was quite possible Briggs was there.

The pit bulls that joined us were rescue dogs, Tash and Boru. They adored Clodagh and Brian and were full of spastic energy. I took some comfort in knowing they'd be coming along, because I truly didn't know what was in store for us. Since the reputation of pit bulls being evil too often mistakenly precedes them, Tash and Boru's very presence would be an added measure of safety.

As we made our way deep into the heart of the city, Memorial Day celebrations turned to empty homes and emptier despair. Josh and I sat in the far back of the van and taped posters to the side walls, ready to grab them and hand off to Clodagh as she jumped out the front door at each street corner. The van cocooned us in its lumbering safety, blocking the sad neighborhood views from our sight. The dogs circled endlessly as we crept along, licking us sometimes, then rushing up to the front to peer over the dashboard.

Turning to gaze through the back window, I watched a woman scream at her half-naked toddler on the sidewalk.

"It just feels so angry here," I said.

And it was true. This place was eerily quiet, simmering with some strange mix of anger and emptiness that clung sullenly to everything and everyone in the neighborhood.

Aside from the chastised toddler, there were no children running around or playing games, no barbecue grills smoking with Johnsonville Brats. It was as if Memorial Day had forgotten this place. The people who *were* outside sat quietly on their porches noting the presence of a van that they didn't recognize creeping down their streets.

We approached a main intersection. With five streets intersecting, it formed awkward angles and offered plenty of street corners. This was prime real estate for dealers and hookers to gather, exchanging insults and laughter. Brian stopped the van here. With his dark hair and tan skin, Brian's ethnicity was indeterminable. He insisted that we stay in the van to cover him. Anxiously, I eyed the groups of bored, drunken young men hanging out on each corner. Brian could easily be just the entertainment they were looking for.

"I don't like this," I said.

"It's fine," Brian said, and with a promise to stay in our line of sight, he got out of the van. As I watched him walk away, I hoped it wasn't a decision we'd come to regret.

We watched as he snaked his way from corner to corner, confidently putting up flyers. His bright green Irish Hurling jersey stood out like a beacon. The dogs pressed against each other, with their paws on the dashboard, low whines emanating from them as they tracked his progress. Then, promptly breaking his promise, Brian disappeared around a corner and out of our sight.

"Oh shit, Brian! Really?"

We all went on high alert, and the minutes ticked by.

"Seriously, what is he doing?" Clodagh unbuckled her seatbelt and started to climb into the driver's seat; belatedly realizing that she should have done that the second that Brian had exited the van.

Josh stood up and moved toward the door, ready to jump out with the dogs if necessary.

"Let's go, Clo," we said.

A flash of bright green caught our eye as Brian rounded the corner. He passed closely by one group of young men and began walking quickly toward the car.

The group turned, and a tall man with a hat pulled low on his forehead broke away from them. He began mimicking how Brian was walking and sped up to get close to him.

Then we saw him reach into his pocket.

Acting on impulse, Josh popped the door open quickly, and the dogs lunged, barking like crazy.

"What the fuck!" The startled man jumped back, then turned tail and ran back to the corner.

"Awwww, shit!" His friends laughed and ribbed him while calling insults to the van, yet noticeably keeping their distance.

Brian hopped into the idling van, and Clodagh squealed away just as Josh swung the door shut.

"What in the hell were you doing back there?!"

"It's fine. I've worked in bad neighborhoods like this all over the country. You just have to act a certain way." Incredibly calm, Brian remained unconcerned that he might have been within an arm's reach of real trouble.

103

"Um, Brian, there was a dude following you, real close, like he was going to jump you," Clodagh said.

"No kidding? Well, I'm still here. No worries."

Blithely moving on, Brian continued directing us towards intersections in the neighborhood until my anxiety reached a new level.

"Can we move a little farther out now?" I asked, no longer willing to put anyone in jeopardy.

As we discussed our next move, my phone began to ring. I had suspected that this neighborhood would generate a whole new batch of hate calls.

"I sliced your dog's fucking neck and let my dogs tear him apart."

And so, just like that, it began again.

The phone calls from children were the worst. Disgusting threats administered from angelic voices was a brutal contradiction. They seemed too young to know such evil. After hanging up on yet another child who politely insisted that he had cut off my dog's tail, I was reluctant to answer the next call on my phone.

"Yeah, yeah. I got information on your dog. Come meet me." The caller was clearly a child, though I was unable to determine how old.

"Excuse me?" I motioned to Josh to have Brian pull the van over.

I listened to the kid as Boru came over and licked my face gently. I stared into his soulful brown eyes and wished I wasn't sitting in the back of a van on a hot summer day, desperately searching for my own sweet-eyed pup. As the child's voice droned in my ear, I swallowed dryly against the rage in my throat. My instincts told me that this child was toying with us. Yet, I had learned just how observant children are. If I ignored this call, I could be taking a chance on missing out on information about Briggs.

Knowing that this was most likely a set-up, I went against my instincts.

"Okay," I heard myself saying to the kid, "we'll meet you. Where do you live?"

After a song and dance about where he really lived, I was able to pull cross streets from him. Deciding to make him work for it, I insisted that he meet us at a McDonald's down the street from where he lived. At the very least, we would be in a very public spot.

"Let's roll," I said when I hung up.

As I'd been smart enough to pull the kid's location from him, we decided to drive there prior to meeting him at McDonald's. We entered a neighborhood of small streets, smaller houses, and groups of people milling around in the road, with no regard for traffic. Laws mattered little in this neighborhood. Turning a corner, we followed a car with a large decal stuck across its back window: "Cocaine Bitch."

Stay classy, Milwaukee, I thought.

The scene, typical for this area, unfolded for us outside of the van window. People clustered in groups on the streets and the sidewalks, passing drugs around casually as they sipped beer. Drinking in public was the least of their concerns.

Dogs were conspicuously missing from this picture.

As our slow-cruising van began to gather more attention, I suggested that we move on to McDonald's. This particular branch of the "Golden Arches" was situated on a busy street of Milwaukee, tucked in a strip mall directly across from a grocery store and a gas station. More than a little concerned that we were being set up, we decided to park across the street from the fast food joint like some kind of stakeout team.

We already had the van, we might as well run some surveillance, I thought. Both the dogs whined quietly, unsure of our plan. We had no answer for them. All we could do was wait and watch.

I laughed at the absurdity of the situation.

"I truly have no idea what to look for. Should we be looking for a kid with Briggs on a leash?"

The kid hadn't given us a name, a description, or anything, but we did notice one young boy who kept circling the lot on his bicycle. I wondered if that was our caller. We decided to drive across the street, and after we parked, Brian got out and did a quick run through of the McDonald's.

Ultimately, the biggest problem was that we had no way of knowing if we were being watched. We couldn't simply interrogate every male adolescent in the parking lot to see if they had called us about a dog. We already had a target on our back by offering a cash reward wherever we went. Follow the wrong lead and we might be sorry. Or worse.

Finally, Brian joined us in the van again.

"I didn't see anything but people ordering food and eating, and no one approached me," he said.

"Let's get out of here," I suggested, as my instincts were telling me that it was just another bullshit call — just one more child thinking it would be fun to mess with us.

Sadly, such is the state of the world — the good, the bad, and the ugly. For every person who stepped up to help us, there were many working against us. We had a choice: we could either let that bitter truth break our faith in humanity, or we could continue to hold on to hope and believe that there is an inherent good in people. We chose to believe in the good, simply because we had to.

Sighing, I refocused on the conversation, which was now centering on areas we had not yet been to. My companion's voices bounced off the van walls, surrounding me in a storm of unanswered questions. My vibrating phone nudged me out of my fog.

"How come you ain't come to the McDonald's?" the kid asked.

"We were there. Where were you?" I said.

"What? You went? Where were you?"

"We were there. Where were you?" I asked again.

"Ha-ha-ha-ha—motherfuckers."

As his uncontrollable laughter filled my ear, I quietly hung up on him.

"It was a setup by a goddamn kid. I knew it. I *knew* it! He thinks this is a joke."

My rage filled the van.

The last of our daylight was gone now.

That night, we sat on the couch and tried to process the weekend's events. From false leads to fake-outs to threatening phone calls, we puzzled over why people were so cruel.

"Okay. I understand being motivated by money and wanting to know about the reward, but why would they threaten to rape me or kill our dog?" I asked. What was the point in threatening me?

Josh thought it was a true reflection of the state of our poor, battered inner city where feelings of anger, hopelessness, and sadness were pervasive. To us, our dog being stolen was a tragedy, but for those in the violence-filled inner city, loss was a daily expectation. Guns, drugs, and trying to get by day-to-day *is* their reality. In the face of that, our despair over a dog was both laughable and an opportunity to make money.

In the worst parts of the city, dogs were often used for more than just protection. Dogs were fighters and moneymakers. While my own personal belief lies somewhere between the death penalty and medieval torture for those who fight dogs, I knew there were people who see dogs as nothing more than expendable objects that they can use to turn a profit.

*Put to fight...put to fight...put to fight...*the phrase echoed through my head.

"Aw, that's too bad 'bout your dog. He probably been put to fight," was said to us so casually over and over throughout the weekend. Just a way of life, right? Fighting dogs to make money, letting them die for a few dollars more. How horrific. How sad. How terrifyingly real.

I thought back to my conversation with the homeless guys in our alley who just so happened to be some of the nicest people I'd ever met. These were my guys — a fountain of information for me. They had their fingers on the pulse of what was really going on in the city because they were out there living in it. As we sat on the couch, I relayed their stories to Josh:

"Yeah, when it comes to a dog like yours, they'll just pull its teeth and throw him in with the big dogs. They make your dog the mark to train their fighters."

"I hear this one guy skins cats and puts 'em in a burlap sack. He keeps 'em alive but lets the blood drip down. That brings out the dogs' killer instincts, and they smell the blood and attack the burlap bag."

"I seen the neighborhood kids walking door to door with their dogs, looking at other dogs, trying to arrange fights."

Josh stated the obvious.

"No wonder everyone there is scared of dogs. They are constantly surrounded by dogs that are trained to fight."

I grew nauseous thinking about Briggs, with his teeth pulled, blood dripping from his mouth, forced into a corner, fighting bigger dogs for his life. That's the problem with the unknown. I had no idea of the truth, and the possibilities sickened me.

Day 13

THE BUZZING OF MY PHONE jerked me awake, the plastic phone vibrating hard against the surface of side table.

"Ugh," I mumbled. I was starting to hate my phone. Being a relatively private person, I rarely gave my phone number out and always used a secondary email address for online shopping, newsletters, and Facebook. Before Briggs' abduction, I never answered calls from unfamiliar or restricted phone numbers.

"Rape, kill, or money?" I muttered crankily as I picked up my phone.

Josh rolled over and glared at me, but said nothing about my macabre sense of humor.

Deflecting the caller who wanted money (of course), I listened to the fifteen messages, all of them hang-ups or requests to know the reward amount. I clicked my phone off, rolled my eyes, stretched, and walked downstairs, with coffee on my mind. Yawning, I blurrily checked the Briggs' Facebook page where I'd updated the followers with the events of our weekend. I nearly dropped my coffee as I saw hundreds of new likes on the page.

Annmarie, making good on her promise, had gotten the word out. Following up on my email from the day before, Annmarie had taken the information I'd sent her and forwarded it to several of her popular on-air personalities. She'd even contacted her network and requested that the Briggs poster be circulated throughout major companies.

Overcome with gratitude, I emailed Annmarie with my heartfelt thanks. I didn't want to disturb her too much, but her quick response to my email showed that she was already devoted to the cause. Soon, our emails were ping-ponging back and forth, filled with suggestions and ideas. Somehow, I'd known from the first moment that I met her that this tiny woman with a big heart and soul-searching eyes would have a huge impact on the Briggs search. Annmarie managed to book us for a spot with a popular midday show, *Marilyn Mee*. Soon thereafter, Marilyn joined the cause, emailing me directly with her own personal suggestions for help. While one of my good high school friends was also a radio morning show host, the infamous "Kidd O'Shea," I was still surprised to be emailing back and forth with another local celebrity. I'd caught her show, and I found it interesting that my perception of her held pretty true or at least via email. My friend Steven, a.k.a. "Kidd O'Shea," had been willing to help with Briggs right off the bat, before anyone in public knew what was going on. It made me smile. Animal lovers come from all walks of life.

Excited and rejuvenated, I dreaded going back to work and my fluorescent cubicle of hell. Our purpose had grown, and I could feel the energy building. Sitting at my desk that day, I watched as a movement grew. My phone was hot to the touch from all the alerts and calls that were forthcoming. Briggs' story was becoming something bigger than all of us.

Annmarie continued to email me throughout the day. She was a brilliant, well-connected woman with a wealth of ideas and suggestions.

"What have you done to reach out to the Hispanic community?" she asked, focused on the eyewitness description.

I told her how we had translated the flyers into Spanish and had canvassed the neighborhoods, food trucks, and grocery stores in the area, but we weren't sure what our other options were, if any.

She went on to explain to me how radio advertising works and said she had a few connections at the smaller Spanish radio stations; she volunteered to look into getting a public service announcement on the air for free.

I over-thanked her and went back to work, my mood lifted. I wondered how it's possible that our little dog was making such a huge impact on people?

As the momentum grew, something inside me began to shrink. The bigger this became, the harder I had to work to contain my emotions; the outpouring of help constantly threatened to bring me to tears.

When Josh came home that night, I could see the same emotional struggle in his eyes. Even worse, he was simultaneously burdened with finding Briggs and trying to protect me. Josh didn't know which was more important at that point: making sure that I didn't burn out, ensuring my personal safety, or finding our dog. Happy with the amount of exposure we had received that day, he gently urged me to sleep.

"Other people are searching for him. You can rest now."

Sleep is a funny thing — a comfort for some. Angst for others. That's the thing about manifesting desires. It fills you up. There isn't much room for pithy life necessities such as sleep. Everything else falls away.

As I lay there, I kept picturing Briggs. Do they know that he loves to play? He's a busy dog who hates to be bored. Boston terriers are known for being active and inquisitive dogs. I hoped that they have toys for him because our house looks like an exploded toy box. I hoped that they knew, and I hoped that they were taking care of him like we would. Like he deserves.

One of Briggs' favorite things to do was to play Frisbee, an absolute obsession of his. If we even said, "Frisbee!" his ears would perk up, and he'd run to the door. Whenever we took him to the dog park, he focused only on that plastic disc. He loved to catch the Frisbee and encourage other dogs to chase him, his ears folded back as he happily tore around the park.

Holding tight to the promise of someday playing Frisbee with Briggs again, I finally drifted into a fitful sleep.

Day 14

A SIX A.M. PHONE CALL startled me out of my restless slumber. A Milwaukee County park ranger's harsh voice tore at me as he demanded that we immediately remove the posters on a popular street that ran the length of the beach on Lake Michigan. It was one of our best spots for high-traffic coverage, as people constantly walked and ran the lakefront. He informed me that the County forbade tape on their light poles, and unauthorized sign postings were prohibited. Angry, I informed this self-righteous security guard that I was under the impression that it was also prohibited to steal a dog off of one's private back deck. I hung up on him, in awe that he would expect us to take down our flyers. We weren't trying to sell anything or scam anyone; we just wanted our dog back.

It had now been two weeks since Briggs' abduction, but it felt like a lifetime. I ignored the park ranger's demand, other than to post the ridiculous exchange on the Briggs' Facebook page. It was kind of fun to read the resulting suggestions of how to handle the park ranger. Our Briggs' community had turned into quite the support system.

Thinking of how far we'd come in only fourteen days, I tried to console myself with the lost dog stories people had told me over the past two weeks. One seemed to linger in my mind: "I heard one dog, Buddy, returned home after two years! Have faith."

Two years? We could not keep this pace up for two years. I knew we were both getting burned out, starting to drag. We would have to throttle back at some point.

But not yet.

"Relentless" was still the name of the game, and it was too soon to stop, too soon to give up. The fact of the matter was that someone had stolen Briggs, and I refused to stop the pressure until the person gave up and gave him back. I prayed that I was making the right decision — that we wouldn't scare this incredibly poor excuse for a human into hurting Briggs.

I am a firm believer in trusting one's instincts, and mine told me to keep pushing. I was beginning to worry people in my life, and annoying the crap out of some — the Milwaukee County park rangers most recently — but I didn't care. Briggs wasn't back home yet.

I checked my list and decided to make a few calls before work. I had been repeatedly calling the company that had sent a crew to wash our windows a few weeks prior. I knew I was offending the owner by asking her to question the Hispanic workers who had come to wash our windows. I pleaded with her to understand that I wasn't accusing her workers; I was simply pointing out that they'd seen Briggs, and perhaps they'd taken a shine to him and spoken to other people about him. I had to keep pushing.

Josh held my hand while I spoke with her.

When I hung up and suggested that we call the roofing company again, Josh said, "Damn it, Tricia, he was a nice guy."

Josh liked the owner of the roofing company, who'd come out to give us a quote the day Briggs was stolen. He had brought his own dog with him, and the dogs had met and played together.

"I'm sorry, babe. I just have to," I said as I dialed the owner. I pled my case, and he understood where I was coming from and realized I had to ask. He was clearly offended, though, so I tried to soften my intent and asked him if he could rack his brain about anything he might have seen that day.

I hated being in this position. No one wants to question someone else's honor. As much as I hated it, though, I had to persist. Next, I called the church and followed up with any workers they'd hired recently. It didn't matter how hard it was for me to make the call; sometimes the difficult questions have to be asked.

With my stomach evolving into a permanent web of knots, I drove into work for the day. Listlessly, I stared at some reports, the numbers blurring in defeat against my distracted brain.

When my phone rang, I looked at the display and was bolstered by the fact that the call wasn't blocked. At the very least, the caller wasn't trying to hide their number. Sad that it's come to that, I thought.

"Hello?" I said, not expecting much.

"Yeah, um, are you looking for a Boston terrier?" A man asked me.

"Yes. Do you have him?" I asked bluntly, and then held my breath.

"Well, I'm not sure. I've got a Boston, but I don't think he's yours. Is yours gray and white?" he asked.

"No. I'm sorry, but ours is black and white. Can you tell me more about the dog? How big is he? Where did you find him?" The questions came tumbling off my tongue. I was on high alert.

"I found him tied to a fence. He's real tiny, about ten pounds. A good-looking little guy, but gray and white, like I said. I just thought he might be yours or that you might be interested in buying him since you like Bostons so much. I can't keep him."

My heart skipped a beat as I tried to process the information. My initial thought was that he had Briggs but was dancing around the truth. That or I was finding out about another stolen dog that was being moved quickly. Not wanting to scare off the caller, I gently asked if he could explain more about how he found the dog, and I mentioned that even if it wasn't Briggs, I might be interested.

For all I knew, there was a dog-stealing ring in Milwaukee, and I'd just stumbled upon a cog in that nasty little wheel.

"Um, I just seen him tied to a fence of an empty house. It looks like they're working on rehabbing the house, but nobody's there, and the dog was just tied up."

"It's crazy that anyone would abandon a dog like that. Do you know what address you got him from? Maybe I could help return him," I said, pretty certain that most people wouldn't just leave a dog tied to a fence.

"Nah, nah. I just want to know if you want to buy him or if you know someone who might. He's real cute. You oughtta see him," he said.

Okay. So this dude's going to dodge all of my questions in an attempt to make a few bucks off of someone else's stolen dog, I thought. Testing him, I asked him for his name.

"My name is Jason," he said.

"Well, Jason, I would certainly be interested, but I'm most interested in finding Briggs, my black and white Boston. You know there's a reward if you find Briggs, right?" I said, realizing I needed to keep Briggs at the forefront of the conversation.

"Yeah, yeah. Me and my cuz be looking for him too. But do you wanna buy this dog, too?" Jason was very focused on getting rid of the dog he had.

"How about this, Jason? Can you send me a picture of this dog, just so that I can make sure it isn't Briggs?"

"Um, I ain't got a picture phone, but the girls next door do. I'll get you one," he said and hung up.

I sat and stared at my phone, overwhelmed. I wanted so very badly for that dog to be Briggs. I prayed that Jason was colorblind and that it was really a black and white Boston terrier. If that were the case, it would be one of our strongest leads to date. Shaking, I quickly texted Josh and waited.

A half an hour later, my phone beeped with an incoming text. It was from an unknown number, but my phone signaled that it was a picture message. Jason had come through.

I took a deep breath and opened the message. The picture was a little blurry but showed a young man in his twenties, presumably Jason, holding a gray and white Boston terrier at arm's length in front of him. The dog was tiny, completely malnourished, with a huge head and eyes that stared straight into my soul.

Calmly, I put my phone down and walked to the bathroom, bypassing the women gossiping at the front desk. I opened the bathroom door and was grateful to find it vacant. I slipped into the handicapped stall and quietly locked the door. As I leaned against the door, I lost it. Everything poured out of me. Tears ran in salty rivers down my cheeks, and I tried to breathe silently so that I wouldn't emit those awful gulping, sobbing sounds that happen when you cry from the very center of your core. My entire body shook with emotion, draining me. I needed it; I hadn't cried since the day Briggs was stolen.

I buried my face in my hands and acknowledged what I had already decided the second my eyes had seen that picture: I needed to save this dog too. I wiped my face and took a deep breath, preparing myself to talk to Jason.

When I returned to my desk, I found that he'd sent several text messages. He wanted to know if I had received the picture and if I wanted the dog.

It was time to negotiate.

I called him back.

"Jason, I need to know where this dog came from," I said flatly.

"Like I told you, I found him tied to a fence. I saved him," he said.

"Why'd you save him if you knew you couldn't keep him?"

"I've got two dogs already, and I thought they'd get along with him okay. The girl don't mind him so much, but my male, Cujo…well, he ain't having it. I guess he ain't keen on havin' two men in the house. Know what I mean?" Jason laughed like we were buddies sharing a joke.

"Sure, I get it. But why didn't you just take him to a shelter?" I asked, as that would have been the obvious course of action to me.

"Nah, I can't do that. I already got money tied up in this dog. I bought a bed, food, a collar. My girl'll be pissed if I don't get that money back."

The picture came into focus: Jason's girlfriend demanded that he make some money off of the dog. Now that I understood, I said, "Okay, Jason, here's the deal. I'll give you seventy-five dollars for him because that's all I've got. The rest of the money is in the reward for Briggs. I want you to look for Briggs, but I'll help this dog in the meantime."

"Seventy-five bucks? C'mon! I can't do that! I need $125."

Continuing in this same manner for half an hour, we finally settled on a fee of $100. The next issue was how to make the exchange. I was understandably reluctant to meet him at his house (truly, as relentless as I was being, I was nowhere near that stupid), so I suggested we meet at a gas station across from a police station after I got off work (the same neighborhood the psychic had predicted — hustling territory), and Jason surprisingly agreed.

With my anxiety gnawing my stomach, I started running through the potential holes in my plan. Am I being set up? Does Jason think he can lure me in with a dog and jump me for the reward money? Steal my car? I had no idea what kind of person I was really dealing with.

Foolishly, I posted the picture on my personal Facebook and asked for advice. Eighty comments later, I quickly removed the post. It was clear to me that quite a few of my friends were ill-equipped when it came to street smarts. I received many useless suggestions that would have made the situation much worse, things like — "Go in with the cops!" While I understood that they were trying to be helpful, they certainly weren't thinking about the bigger picture. If Briggs was still in that neighborhood, the last thing I needed to do was ruin our reputation on the streets by surprising Jason with an ambush from the cops.

On the flipside, I was concerned about the message that I would potentially be sending. Would I be advertising that we were willing to pay cash for all Boston terriers that are "found?" The last thing I needed was for word to get out that I would pay for stolen dogs.

It was a decidedly fine line to walk, and one I did not relish navigating. Trusting my instincts, I deleted the picture and all the comments from Facebook and told everyone that I'd keep them posted. I appreciated the fact that they cared, but it was clear that some people just didn't get it. Luckily, before I removed it, the posting piqued the interest of a few friends I hadn't spoken with in a while. I would later find out that they had set up their own systems of protecting me, unbeknownst to me.

I reached out to Annmarie and sent her the picture of the Boston and told her about my arrangements with Jason.

She immediately responded, "You have to get this dog."

"I know."

She agreed to go with me, and we decided to meet at the CVS and go together. She contacted her husband and filled him in, and I did the same with Josh.

Next, I called my friend Paulie.

"Can you come tonight?" I asked.

After a long-winded rant about opportunists and people who will use any opportunity to make a buck, Paulie agreed to be there to protect us should anything go down.

I was grateful, and I managed to breathe a little easier. Things are going to be okay, I told myself. We're going to save a puppy.

I raced home from work, quickly changed into nondescript clothing, and rushed to meet Annmarie at the CVS. On the way, I received several text messages from Jason. It appeared as though he had done some research in his downtime, and now he wanted to up the ante.

"I looked these dogs up, and they real expensive. I want $500."

I laughed. Hustlas gonna hustle, I thought to myself. Unfortunately for Jason, he had no idea who he was dealing with. I had long ago learned not to negotiate with people like this.

"Sorry, Jason, but $100 is all I have. Cash is yours. You can have it right now," I said into the phone, then sat in my car and waited.

"No, these dogs are pricey. Come look at him. You'll see he worth it."

"No. It's $100 or nothing," I replied flatly.

Silence.

I texted Paulie: "Abort mission. Jason is pulling out. Thanks for being there."

I knew then that it wasn't going to happen, and Jason would try to sell this dog elsewhere. Sighing, I pulled into the CVS parking lot and waited for Annmarie who pulled up shortly thereafter.

Looking stylish in her jeans and leather jacket, Annmarie approached me and gave me a hug.

"Jason is out," I said.

"What?!" she asked furiously.

"He wants $500 for the dog, and I am not paying that. He'll have to come down."

"Well, let's drive around and see if he calls back," Annmarie said.

I agreed, grabbed my mace, flyers, and tape, and got into her car. I figured we might as well do some canvassing if we weren't going to pick up a dog. We cruised slowly past the meeting point to look for signs of Jason, but nobody was there.

My phone buzzed.

"I'll take $450, no less. He's a purebred."

So it's going to be like that? I thought.

"Tell Jason he should be ashamed of himself, that he should do the right thing and save a dog," Annmarie was vocal in her anger at Jason.

I texted her reply and waited for the response.

"I did! I saved the dog. He would've died without me." Apparently, despite his inability to honor a deal, Jason nonetheless considered himself a good Samaritan.

"Listen, Jason, you found the dog in a sketchy way. You have no papers for the dog, and everyone is going to think he is stolen. Good luck trying to sell him. I'll take him off your hands, but it is $100 or nothing," I texted back and held my breath. I was worried that the mention of the dog being stolen would send him running.

"No, miss, I don't steal! He is not stolen! I saved him! $450."

"No. It's $100 or nothing."

"$400?"

"No. Good luck trying to sell him when the entire city of Milwaukee is looking for a stolen Boston terrier. I've got $100 if you want it."

"No, only $400."

"Good luck, Jason." Silently staring out the window, I prayed that I hadn't miscalculated my strategy.

"He'll come back to you, you know," Annmarie said, sounding entirely certain.

"I know," I said.

We continued to drive around, trying to highlight the neighborhood the psychic had detailed in his email. Annmarie stopped at pinpointed locations and gazed silently out of the window. I wondered what she was thinking when she sat there so intensely like that.

We stopped in front of a holistic health store and noticed a woman standing out front, speaking with a homeless man. I got out of the car and handed them flyers.

"She really cared," Annmarie stated when I climbed back in the car.

"Oh yeah? How do you know?"

"I just do."

As we drove around, Annmarie began to question me about the psychics, and I explained my encounters with them. Annmarie nodded as she listened.

"My mother was psychic. She collected the odd, the weird, and filled our house with all kinds of people, from whackos to the real deal." Annmarie stated this casually as she stared out the window at a building.

"Whoa! Really? Was *she* the real deal?"

"Yes. Sadly, she didn't handle it well. Truth be told, everyone in my family has psychic abilities."

As the words registered, I looked at her more closely.

"Everyone? Even you?" I asked.

"I have a gift, strong psychic abilities, but I never use it for personal gain," she said, focusing on the road ahead.

I wondered if she was worried that I would judge her. Secretly, I was a little jealous. Ecstatic, my mind filled with a zillion questions. All of a sudden, I felt like I had my own secret weapon in the Briggs hunt. Cautiously, I let her know that I thought it was an amazing gift and told her I was very interested in learning how it worked for her. Frankly, I didn't care if she could read every thought in my head. At that point, I was happy to use every tool offered to me for the Briggs hunt.

As we drove around, Annmarie explained that she occasionally saw flashes of things or could read people and know whether or not they were telling the truth. At times, she could predict events or foresee when bad things were going to happen. She said it just happened on its own; she couldn't summon any of those abilities on command.

Amazed, slightly in awe, and utterly impressed, I could only nod. I'd met people with psychic abilities before, yet she was perhaps the most believable person that I had ever met when it came to extra-sensory gifts.

"Is that why you came to our doorstep?" I wondered out loud.

"Absolutely. Tricia, you have no idea how many people ask me for help every day in my position at work. It is difficult to turn people down, but oftentimes I have to. Your cause touched me in a few different ways, and I had to reach out to help you."

Annmarie then went on to explain that she'd seen my email to the radio station, yet had dismissed it at the time. She received hundreds of emails a day, so many that they were difficult to keep up with. That same day, she had seen our poster at Starbucks, and later that night, she was at dinner with her husband in the 4000 block of Oakland Avenue.

"I walked across the street to see what the vegetarian options were at another restaurant and saw your flyer. It slammed me in my gut. When I returned to the restaurant where my husband was, I saw another flyer on the door. I couldn't look away from it. The emotion was so powerful," Annmarie said. We had reached her four times in one day, and she decided it was time to act.

"Those were the first flyers we put up," I said, amazed. I recalled the first night — the night the ragtag group of psychics had directed me to put flyers on that block. All of the sudden, it made sense. Briggs wasn't at the 4000 block, but help was.

"I could feel it. Total sadness just hit me when I saw the poster, as well as great anger. I kept staring at it over dinner. I couldn't even eat. I asked the waitress for more information, but she hadn't even noticed the flyer." Annmarie went on to detail how distracted and upset she was throughout dinner and on their way home. Her husband, knowing her well, had looked at her and asked if they should go back for the information.

"I have to. I have to go see them," she told him. They then went back for her to gather our information, and their next stop was our doorstep.

"I wanted to read you," she explained. "I wanted to see if you were the real deal, if what I was sensing from the poster was true emotion."

"Now I know why I felt like you were staring into my soul," I said, "and, why, for some reason, I felt instantly bonded to you."

"I knew it was wrong to show up on your doorstep like that, strangers in the dark, and I was sure it would frighten you. I'm sorry about that, but I had to. I could feel how sad Josh was too," Annmarie said.

"I wasn't going to put our address on those flyers, but something compelled me to, even against my better judgment."

As we mulled it all over, we continued cruising neighborhoods, periodically getting out and handing flyers to children who tended to be far more observant than most adults. I told Annmarie that I'd seen a mother and child walk past my car, and the child kept pulling his mom's arm and trying to drag her back to show her the stolen poster in my back window, but she kept going, disinterested.

My phone buzzed yet again. This time, it was text message from my friend Peter. He wanted to know how things had worked out. After I filled him in, he agreed with my stance to avoid negotiations with Jason. Later, I would come to find out that Peter had stationed people at all corners of the intersection, with instructions to keep an eye on us. If anything had gone down, we would have been covered.

Again, I knew that kind of support couldn't be bought. Grateful for my friends, I went home to continue our nightly online campaign and fill our followers in on what had happened with Jason. Recalling Annmarie's suggestion that we needed to focus on the Hispanic communities, I began work on a Spanish website dedicated to Briggs. If we did manage to get a blurb on the Hispanic radio stations, it would be important to have a place to direct the listeners, and phone numbers would be difficult for people to remember or jot down while they were driving and listening to the radio.

My friend Matt and I worked late that night to get a site up and running for Spanish-speakers. I purchased a URL, www.leechodemenosmiperro.com
(www.imissmydog.com), which would be easy for listeners to remember. The site was really nothing elaborate and was simply a Spanish version of the poster, translated by my friend Jessica, but it felt good to know it was up and running.

Matt, bona fide computer geek that he was, proved to be an invaluable resource to our hunt. From helping with the website to continually spreading the word, he was something like my social media campaign publicist. He continued to give me daily progress reports, and was I blown away that Twitter was all a flurry with the Briggs poster, even though I wasn't on Twitter myself.

"This is how you know you're good at marketing, Tricia. You didn't even have to be on Twitter to get the word out. Twitter followed *you*."

Day 15

A FULL TWO WEEKS HAD passed. Time was now broken down into hours, minutes, and seconds; we'd come to learn that that was just how quickly our lives could change.

I checked my phone and saw a text from Amy, a friend, animal advocate, and all-around good person. She wanted to know if she should have her friend, an animal psychic, try to make contact with Briggs. Unsure, but at this point open to anything, I told her to go ahead.

Amy was a bit worried though. "What if she finds out something bad? I don't know if I would be able to tell you."

"No matter how bad the news, you won't be telling me anything I haven't already thought about," I said.

An hour or two later, I received an email from her: "I'm so sorry I have to forward this on, but if it can help in any way, then I have to do my part."

Gathering my courage, I read on: "I was able to make contact with Briggs. He is terrified. He is lying on a narrow concrete dog run, looking through a chain-link fence. He is scared to come out of the corner. He keeps asking when his mom is coming to pick him up. I told him you are looking for him, and that makes him happy."

After my emotional breakdown the day before, I knew the last thing I needed to do was lose it again. Nevertheless, my eyes blurred as I reread the words: "Terrified...when his mom is coming to pick him up..." I shut off my laptop and somehow managed to keep from throwing up. The image of Briggs lying on concrete, terrified was burned into my mind.

To be fair, I had no idea whether I really believed any of this or not. Truth be told, I kind of wanted to punch her for telling me that Briggs was asking for me to come get him. That wasn't right; she could have tailored that for a far less dramatic impact.

"We're coming for you, Briggs," I said.

I wished I could call work and take the day off, but I couldn't. I had no idea how long the situation would go on. There was no way to gauge how many days off I'd need, and I didn't want to use them up too early.

As if on cue, the minute I arrived at work, my phone went ballistic. Briggs' story had gone viral again. Thanks to Annmarie, all the major radio stations in town were talking about Briggs. He was the dog of the day on *Marilyn Mee*, 106.1 shared his story, another DJ contacted me through Facebook and put it on his work blog, Connie and Curtis (radio personalities) shared his poster, and even Kirk, Annmarie's husband and owner of Hal's Harley Davidson, put the poster directly on their website. Overwhelmed and eternally grateful, I answered each and every call without regard to work.

An old high school friend of mine contacted me through Facebook. Kristy had originally reached out and offered to call vets for us when Briggs was first stolen, but now she was calling to let me know she'd contacted Carolyn Gracie of QVC, and Carolyn had generously agreed to share the Briggs poster on her page.

Briggs had gone national. Again.

Ecstatic, I answered a call from a woman named Shonda who had seen a Boston terrier at a house on 36th street. It wasn't exactly in the best part of town, but I was determined to go check it out after work.

Annmarie wanted in, and because her car was in the shop, she picked me up after work in a bright red rental, not the most inconspicuous car for a stakeout. I filled her in on the psychic's message and what Shonda had told me about seeing a Boston in the front yard of a home on 36th. Annmarie didn't immediately dismiss what the animal communicator had said, but she did wish there'd been more information — like the name of a street, for instance.

As we headed deeper into the city, my eyes scanned the streets and alleyways, looking for a dog, a chain-link fence, anything.

Luckily, Shonda had described the house clearly. We cruised slowly past it since it wasn't the kind of street to stop and set up surveillance on. We circled and went through the back alley, creeping along. As we rolled through, tension gripped me, and I kept looking behind me. My skin was crawling. We were glaringly out of place, and it was being noted.

We circled a couple more times before pulling into a spot on the same street, across from a Cricket store. At the very least, we might look like customers shopping for a pre-paid "burner" phone.

Annmarie watched the nondescript, run-down two-story house. A chain-link fence surrounded the minimal scrap of yard littered with trash and a few toys. I looked at those broken, old, filthy toys and wondered about the children who lived there. Would they be kind to a dog? My mind started wandering down all the horrible stories I had heard recently:

"We brought a cat in today that was rescued from a group of kids that were starting to skin it alive."

"We rescued a dog today. Some kids cut off his ear."

Shoving those grim possibilities from my head, I focused on the rearview mirror. Mace in hand, I wanted to be prepared if someone snuck up on us.

"The door's opening," Annmarie said.

My emotions went into overdrive. Hypersensitive, I watched, desperately praying to catch a glimpse of Briggs, but at the same time, hoping I wouldn't. I knew if I saw him, I wouldn't be able to hold myself back from running over to get him.

Situations like that revealed how grossly unprepared I was to handle an actual confrontation. Logically, I knew I'd have to approach in a calm, smart, reasonable manner. Still, I was fairly certain that if it came down to it, my mace would be doing the talking for me. Knowing that you have to approach a situation rationally versus actually seeing your dog and trying not to attack the — those were two different things.

As I mentally reviewed what I would do if Briggs came out (go for the junk, Tricia!), I watched a young man leave the yard, lock the fence, get in a car, and drive away. There was no sign of Briggs.

We quickly discussed our options. Should we go up, ring the bell, and listen for a dog barking? The trouble was that the man had locked his fence, and this was not the neighborhood to randomly be knocking on doors.

Defeated, I texted Shonda and thanked her, filling her in on what we had seen. She promised to drive by later with her husband and said she'd have her daughter drive that way to work each day. It felt good to know that someone would be there, on neighborhood watch, keeping an eye out for our dog.

We decided to head down to the South Side and use the rest of the daylight to put up flyers. We were reluctant to go into the dive bars and instead focused on churches, liquor stores, and schools.

At a bus stop, I handed a flyer to an elderly woman who had her hair wrapped against the promise of rain.

She kindly took it and asked, "Qué es esto?"

Realizing that she spoke no English, I switched to my limited Spanish.

"Buscando mi perro."

"Su perrito?"

"Sí, sí."

"El tiene un pata blanca." I pointed to his white sock in the picture.

She smiled kindly, blessed me, and tucked the flyer in her purse. I found something oddly comforting about her blessing.

Pleased with how I'd handled the Spanish interaction, we moved on to more stops. The misty, gray day finally fulfilled its promise of rain, and fat drops began to fall. This made it increasingly difficult to put up flyers.

Standing in front of a school, I prayed the tape would hold. The psychic had said Briggs was with small children at night, and I could only hope a child would see his picture and tell someone.

We admitted defeat against the weather, and Annmarie drove me home. Just as she parked in front of my house, a car full of Hispanic-looking boys pulled up. With our systems on full alert, we sat in the car and waited, watching, wishing that we'd see Briggs' happy ears perk up. The rain made it hard to see clearly, and questions began to swirl through my brain. Who are these guys? Why is their car running? As the light grew darker, it became even more difficult to see what they were doing. When we heard a door slam, I turned to see a girl leaving the apartment building across the street, heading to the car. I had to laugh a little and admit that I had perhaps become too suspicious for my own good.

When I entered our lifeless house, I wished for the thousandth time that Josh didn't have to work second shift. With trepidation in my heart and mace in my pocket, I slowly climbed the stairs to the third floor, running through lists in my head. I signed on to Facebook and updated all the followers about the day's progress. My inbox was overloaded with 257 new messages. Going viral was a lot of work, I thought.

As I read through the emails, I tried not to become overwhelmed with all the ideas.

"Have you tried this? Have you tried…have you done…have you gone…have you thought of…?"

It all began to swim in front of my eyes. Forcing myself to breathe deeply, I tried to get a grip on the monumental task ahead. For every idea we had tried, every place we'd already gone, there were hundreds of places we hadn't even touched. While I understood that the email suggestions were simply meant to be helpful, in an odd way they were making me feel inadequate, as if I wasn't doing enough.

In my head, it was beginning to sound more like, "Why haven't you tried this yet?"

I forced myself to focus, knowing no good could come from self-inflicted negativity. I continued to take notes, thank people, and responded to emails relentlessly until Josh got home.

After we recapped our day, we silently readied ourselves for bed. The time for words was gone. Talked out and exhausted, we curled up and silently held each other as we stared into the darkness.

Day 16

FRIDAY DAWNED EARLY FOR ME with the incessant, painfully familiar buzzing of my phone. Josh was asleep peacefully next to me, his dreams uninterrupted. As someone who instantly wakes up at any noise and can't fall back asleep easily, I saw no point in ignoring my phone.

Reaching over, I squinted at it and smiled. Our friend Jason was back. I had known it was a gamble to refuse to negotiate price with him, but I had gone with my gut, and my instincts had proven correct.

"I can't keep this dog. You got $225?" asked the text.

Well, that's a drastic price cut, I thought.

"Sorry, Jason. I just want Briggs," I texted, biting my lip and praying I was not screwing that poor little dog's life up and that my ploy would work.

"I can't find anyone to take him. Please. $200." Jason's desperation was apparent.

"Jason, I want Briggs. Have you heard anything about him?"

"No. My cuz and I be searching, but we ain't heard nothing."

"Jason, you had your chance at $100. That was it."

"Man, come on! Just $200. You gotta see this dog. He's a good-looking dog. I looked him up. Blue and white Bostons are real special. This is a deal."

"No, I don't want to see him. I want Briggs."

My phone went quiet.

Hoping that I'd played this correctly and that Jason would come back to our original deal, I got out of bed and snatched my laptop. I emailed my main crew of street warriors, filling them in on the developments.

After mulling the situation over, I decided to update the Briggs Facebook page. At that point, the followers had become as much of the story as anyone else, and they already knew about Jason from a post earlier that week. If I did manage to get the little gray and white dog from him, I wanted to make sure that the word was out. My suspicion was that he'd been stolen, and the more people who knew about it, the more likely we would be to find his owners.

The flood of comments followed shortly:

"Go get him!"

"Save that pup! We'll help you find his home!"

"I can foster him if you need me to!"

Bolstered by the comments, I felt confident that we could handle whatever came our way that day — until I checked my voicemail.

"Have you ever considered that maybe you just *lost* your dog? And have you ever considered answering your phone so people can help you? I mean, not me, 'cause I can't," an annoying voice rang out at me from my phone, followed by the dial tone.

Amazed at the complete disrespect of some people, I immediately posted that delightful message to Facebook. And I admit it was nice to see other people were just as enraged as I was over this brand of calls. I felt Josh's arm circle me as I angrily typed, and then he rested his head on mine.

"You okay?"

Silently, I nodded.

Deciding to make use of our daylight time together, Josh and I picked a neighborhood to canvas before he had to go into work. While we were incredibly grateful for social media and the ability to share information quickly, we were finding out that our flyers were reaching the kind of people we needed to reach.

My phone buzzed with a text message, a picture from Jason. I opened it and gulped back tears as I stared into the face of the puppy whose head was too big for his body. He leaned a little, off kilter, tied to a dirty deck. His huge head was in decided contrast to his rail-thin body, and ribs poked out from his matted fur. His eyes stared dully at me, begging me for help.

"What are you going to do with him when you get him?" Josh asked, knowing me too well.

"Feed him and find him a home…and keep looking for Briggs." One thing I would not allow was for that dog to distract us from finding ours.

"Mm-hmm." Not only did Josh know me well enough to know how quickly I formed attachments to animals, but he also knew when to keep some of his thoughts about me to himself. Josh knew me well enough to not voice his thoughts: "She'll keep this dog in a heartbeat if it needs help."

I had to be honest with myself; I would save all the dogs in the world if I could. Any animal, for that matter. I've always had a strong affinity for animals. Oftentimes, I found that when I had difficulties communicating with people, animals were a strong source of comfort. I think that's why so many people love animals. They provide companionship, loyalty, understanding, and comfort without judgment; attributes that few people offer one another. The truth of it is that I like most animals more than many of the people I've met in my life.

"Keep me posted…and don't do anything stupid," Josh warned, breaking into my thoughts. "I'm serious. I can't go to work thinking you might end up in a stand-off in the hood, trying to rescue some dog."

"What! Crazy. No, of course not," I said, unable to look him in the eyes.

Smiling a bit, he kissed me gently and left for work.

Okay, Jason. Let's play ball, I thought to myself as I contacted my backup.

"Code Red. Code Red. Jason is back and willing to negotiate. I wouldn't be surprised if he comes down in price. Will one of you go with me today if he does?" I asked them.

Several texts bounced back in response: Annmarie after six o'clock, Megan in the late afternoon, and Paulie might, if he was back in town in time.

Once I got an idea of timeframe for my backup, I responded to Jason.

"Aw, he certainly is cute. Have you heard anything about Briggs?"

"Naw, I be looking. Me and my cuz look. Miss, do you want this dog? I been calling him Diesel. He's real sweet."

"Listen, Jason, You had your offer — $100. You said no. The offer still stands."

"I need $200. Please. You gotta see him. This is a show dog."

"Jason, you can't sell this dog in Milwaukee. You know you can't because you clearly tried this week. Everybody is on the lookout for a Boston. You're stupid to ask for more. If you need money, mine's the best offer you're gonna get."

"I can't, my girlfriend be pissed if I don't get money back."

"I highly doubt that dog food and a collar cost you $200 this week."

"It did! I swear. I bought a bed too."

"Uh-huh. I told you $100."

"What about $175?"

Phew, I thought, glad he was finally budging. As negotiations continued, I became increasingly tense. Was I committing this dog to a horrible outcome by not just agreeing to Jason's price?

"Just come look at him. You'll see that he's a good-looking dog."

A fool I was not. That was the last thing I was going to do. Obviously, I'd fall in love with the puppy if I saw him in person and lose all ability to negotiate. A price had to be decided ahead of time. Hours later, I finally negotiated Jason down.

"Lady, $125. Please. I really need it."

"Fine," I agreed, if and only if he promised to take the flyers of Briggs and to contact me immediately if he heard anything on the streets. I wanted him to know that the real money was in finding Briggs.

Jason agreed to meet me at the gas station again. Frantic, I knew I had to move quickly. The last time I'd given Jason too long to think he had backed out. I did not want to lose that dog again.

Only Megan could go with me, it being four o'clock on a Friday afternoon. Extremely nervous, she peppered me with questions on her way over to pick me up. Understanding her concern, I told her I'd call the police station across the street and speak with an officer before we met with Jason.

"Sir, I'm about to purchase a dog from a man at the gas station across the street," I explained to the officer on the phone and gave him a rundown of the transaction.

"Really? That gas station gets robbed almost weekly. Probably not the smartest move," the officer said, his sarcasm almost dripping through the phone.

Ahem. Well then.

"Um, what do you suggest?"

"I suggest you have him meet you here. If the dog isn't stolen, he shouldn't have a problem with it."

Fair enough. I let him know we were on our way and to keep an eye out for us. He agreed. I could all but hear him thinking, *stupid girl.*

I decided to wait until we were en route before I asked Jason to meet me at the police station. Megan picked me up, and I took a towel with me, ready to wrap the puppy up. Having no idea of his condition, I was scared that he would transmit fleas or something worse to Megan's own Bostons. I instructed her to head toward the police station, placed my mace in the cup holder, and picked up my phone.

"Meet us at the police station instead, across the street. On our way." I sent the text and held my breath, praying that Jason wouldn't hassle us.

Located on a side street, the police station was situated directly across from a row of dilapidated houses. I couldn't help noticing that we were smack dab in the middle of one of the neighborhoods that the psychic had told us Briggs might be in. I silently wondered if this was still the case, or if they'd moved him. Megan waited in the car as I paced the sidewalk.

I stared down every car that drove by, intently looking for the telltale ears of a Boston terrier. The minutes ticked by. Cars pulled up, and people got out, but I saw no dogs. A thought occurred to me: am I a sitting duck standing out on the sidewalk by myself? No. I knew I wasn't. Instinctively, I knew that Jason wasn't out to hurt me. He was just an opportunist looking to cash in.

My phone rang, and Jason asked, "Yeah, why you ain't at the gas station?"

Breathing a sigh of relief, I told him that the girl I was with felt more comfortable meeting by the police station and that I was standing outside, waiting for him.

"A'ight. I be over."

Two minutes later, a battered red Trans Am turned the corner, sped up, whipped a U-turn, and parked across from me. The infamous Jason had arrived. A tall, good-looking man in his mid-twenties, Jason was dressed in a matching Adidas tracksuit and shoes. Stretching out his lanky frame, he casually crossed the street, cradling the tiny puppy under his arm.

Nervous, I smiled at him before he reached me and immediately cooed, "Aw, he is really tiny," trying to radiate as much kindness and goodwill as I could muster.

I reached for the puppy quickly; I was terrified that Jason would step back and hold him out of my reach. Luckily, he handed him over right away, and I passed him the folded wad of cash. Looking down into the dog's eyes, I simply melted inside. He stared up at me with utter conviction, and then stretched up until he could sniff my face.

147

Giving me a singular lick with his abrasive little tongue, he settled back into the crook of my arm.

"Wow, I ain't see him do that before," Jason exclaimed.

"Really?" I asked, surprised, since puppies tend to lick and love up on everyone. I wondered what had been going on at Jason's house that the puppy didn't feel comfortable showing that type of affection.

"Yeah, he's kinda grown on me actually. I been taking him everywhere with me, since he can't be in the house with Cujo. Man, Cujo ain't having it, that's for sure."

"Is that so?" Unsure of how to respond to that statement, I simply cuddled the puppy.

"Yeah, little Diesel's a good dog. Please take care of him." And with that, Jason loped across the street and was gone, but my phone buzzed immediately with a text from him.

"Please send me pics if you keep him. Take care of him."

So, I thought with a smile, this little pup had wormed his way into the hustler's heart, after all. Thinking of my next steps, I pulled the towel out of the car, wrapped him up, and sat down.

"Oh my God!" Megan squealed. "He is so freaking cute. Oh my God! So…tiny!"

She was right about that, and the little rescue pup (I refused to call him Diesel) just kept staring at me, only looking around a little bit. Jason was right. He was a beautiful dog. I spoke to him in mindless, soothing words — anything to let the little guy know that he was safe.

Megan dropped me off, and I thanked her profusely. Not everyone has the guts to go through with that little mission we'd just pulled. I've always admired a strong backbone in a woman.

"Okay, buddy, stay with me. We have to get you checked out."

Keeping him wrapped in the towel, I immediately went to my car, hoping I'd make it to the emergency vet while they were still open. I knew if he'd been microchipped, we could find his rightful owners, if he had any. For all I knew, Jason's story was true, and the rescue pup really was an abandoned dog.

The puppy nestled in. He didn't cry, didn't whimper, and didn't squirm around. He just sat quietly in my lap, fitting easily between me and the steering wheel, and continued to stare up at me in complete and utter faith.

"You're safe now." Crooning it over and over, I patted him gently.

Relieved that I'd made it in time, I let the rescue puppy out on the grass by the vet to do his business. When he was finished, I scooped him up and took him into the clinic, all the while debating how I was going to explain the situation without flat out saying that I might have just paid for a stolen dog.

Much to my surprise and delight, after I delicately explained the situation, the vet's office agreed to check him over for free. My little rescue, on the other hand, was far less impressed with the free exam and began to shake uncontrollably.

"It's okay. I'm not leaving you here. I promise," I said to him over and over.

Trembling, he kept staring up at me. I was surprised by his complete focus on me. Most puppies I'd met were a bit roly-poly and all over the place. I could tell that he had gone through some rough times in his young life, but just how rough had yet to be determined.

"Are you Briggs' owner?" a woman asked as she stepped out from the back.

"Yes, I am," I said, assuming the receptionist had filled her in.

"Oh my goodness! I've been following your story. You should know I've shared your story with many people, and we're all rooting for you. How good of you to rescue this guy too."

"Thanks! Every share helps, and we really appreciate all you're doing." Cuddling the rescue puppy, I walked back into the exam room.

The vet came in, a pretty lady with smiling eyes.

"So, what exactly is the story here?"

I filled her in, and she pulled out the wand to scan him.

Holding my breath, I prayed for…well, truth be told, I prayed there wasn't a microchip. I'd already formed quite a bond with the little rescue dog, which came as a shock, even to me. Though I truly did not have the time or energy to nurse him back to health, and I knew that I needed to focus entirely on Briggs, a part of me wanted to keep the little rescue.

"No chip," the vet proclaimed.

The puppy looked at me. Shaking to near convulsions, his little body looked even smaller on the large exam table. He was a beautiful gray color, but his coat was dull and matted. His large head seemed to droop under its own weight, and his ribs stuck out precariously.

Sighing and clicking her tongue in a *tsk-tsk* way, the vet proceeded to examine him.

"Well, aside from what looks like serious dehydration and malnutrition, this little fella's in surprisingly good shape. I think a bath, some healthy food, and a little comfortable rest will do wonders for him."

"Really?" I said. "No fleas or cuts or anything?"

"Nope. Just some TLC, and he should be up and running."

Relieved, I bundled the puppy back in the towel, more than ready to take him home and figure out what to do next.

Carrying him inside, I said, "Okay, buddy. This is your temporary new home. You'll be safe here."

In a sentimental move, we had left Briggs' water dish out and refilled it daily. Almost to say, "We know you'll be home soon." I put the puppy on the floor, and he looked up at me with his big, overweight head, and then ran to the water dish. His entire body shook as he gulped the water desperately.

"Whoa, boy! Slow down." I gently pulled him away, but he fought me and returned to the water dish and gulped. I pulled him away again, and his tiny body shook. He hung his head and water started pouring back out of his mouth.

He wasn't throwing up, I realized. He had literally drunk his small body to capacity, and the water was overflowing out of his desperate little mouth. The puppy's head drooped, and water continued to pour out. Ashamed, he wouldn't look at me and continued to tremble.

I sat down on the floor with him.

"It's okay, it's okay," I murmured.

He walked over to me and tried to crawl in my lap, and I gently held him as he threw up everywhere.

"It's okay."

Slipping through my grasp, he ran back to the bowl and gulped more water. Then he turned around and promptly threw up again.

"Oooookaay, buddy. Simmer down. Let's take this a little at a time."

After I restricted his water and hand-fed him very small amounts of food, he finally settled down a bit. I sat on the kitchen floor with him, and he curled into my lap, silently staring up at me.

"Shit. You are totally bonded already," I said, not sure if I was talking more to him or to myself. I then sent pictures to Josh and Annmarie.

"I'll be over right after dinner to see him!" Annmarie declared.

Josh texted, "Just don't get too attached, all right? We don't know what the situation is."

"I don't think I'm the one who's attached. He's totally bonded to me."

"Of course he is. He's a puppy."

"No, Josh. This is something deeper. I just know."

Used to his wife being slightly nuts when it came to animals, Josh again withheld comment and said he would see me when he got home. I cuddled the miniature Boston and promised to do everything to keep him safe.

In the meantime, I knew I needed to keep following leads on Briggs. I hopped online and informed the Facebook world of the safe acquisition of the rescue puppy. Hundreds of comments flooded the page with recommendations of what I should do with him. Quickly realizing that putting the rescue puppy's picture up could put him in harm's way, I deleted it from the page. It had been brought to my attention that people were known to lie and say that a lost puppy was theirs simply by describing it from a picture they had seen on the Internet. The last thing we needed was to deliver that poor, malnourished, shaky puppy into the wrong hands.

My phone rang. It was Annmarie letting me know that she was across the street at a pizza parlor and wanted to come over with Kirk to meet the rescue.

"Come on, buddy. Let's go outside and wait for them."

As we sat outside, the rescue pup sniffed the air tentatively. He ventured a few steps out and then quickly returned to the safety and warmth of my lap. It was new territory for him.

Annmarie and Kirk soon made their way across the street to our house. Both were animal lovers and understood the need to approach the puppy with a gentle demeanor. Kirk, with his strong shoulders and white beard, exuded a masculine confidence, coupled with a gentle love for animals. The three of us sat on the grass as dusk fell. The puppy slowly approached them, growled, and bounced back to me.

"Come inside," I said. Inviting them in for the first time, I carried the rescue dog to the kitchen floor. I sat down and cradled the rescue pup in my lap, and Kirk and Annmarie sat next to me. What a surreal moment, I thought. Who are these people sitting on my kitchen floor on a Friday night? The owner of a large company and the head of several major radio stations were curled up on my kitchen floor, gently whispering to the rescue dog, encouraging him to approach. I felt as though I had known them forever.

Wobbling on weak legs, the rescue puppy made his way over to Annmarie. With false bravado, he barked at her, drawing a laugh. In terror, he skidded back to my lap, vibrating and barking.

"He's protecting you and thinks you're the safe zone," Kirk observed.

"I know." I was quiet — too quiet. Trying to keep my emotions in check was really hard, and it was useless to hide anything from Annmarie who could read me from a mile away. Looking down at the puppy, I tried to hold back my tears.

"You aren't giving up on Briggs by rescuing him, you know that, right?" Annmarie asked me.

"Yes, I know."

"Don't feel guilty about rescuing this dog. You have enough love in you to save him and still bring Briggs home. You can do this, Tricia," Annmarie said, seeing straight to the core of things, yet again.

"I do feel incredibly guilty, like I've given up on Briggs or something. I'm scared that caring for the puppy will take away from my search. I don't know how to save them both." That really was the crux of it all. That tiny puppy, shaking and growling in my lap, already looked at me like I was his savior. Would I have it in me to break his heart and give him away?

"You aren't giving up on Briggs," Annmarie said. "You're far too strong to do that. You'll figure out how to make this work. For tonight, you saved one dog. Tomorrow, you can decide what to do with him."

As Annmarie talked me down, I tried to acknowledge the truth of her words. I tried not to cry as I watched Kirk make faces and cooing noises at the rescue puppy. I loved how the puppy tilted his head back and forth curiously at the noises.

Annmarie stood up and walked around the house, stepping out on the deck to take a look at the place where Briggs had been stolen. She was trying to get a read on the man who had taken Briggs and to see if she could pick up any other residual information.

"I don't like this place."

Not one to pull her punches, Annmarie went on to talk about the negative energy on the deck and said she felt like the dognapper might have just been completely emotionally ignorant — as in, he saw a dog he wanted and simply took it, without any thought of our pain or the ramifications of his actions.

"If that's the case, I hope they're at least taking care of him," I said.

After saying their goodbyes, Annmarie hugged me for an extra long moment. "You can do this. You did a good thing today."

"So did you," I said. Annmarie had insisted on covering the $125 for the rescue puppy.

After they left, I curled up on the couch and waited for Josh, contemplating our next move. The rescue stretched out next to me on his back, tummy up, softly snoring. At least I knew he felt safe with me; no dog who felt threatened would sleep like that. Already sensing that we'd encounter some trouble when Josh got home, I texted Josh to come in and sit next to me on the couch when he got home so I could put my arms around him and show the puppy that Josh was part of the family.

As I suspected, the rescue pup shot off the couch and barked incessantly when Josh walked through the door.

"Come over here," I said, smiling at Josh and patting the seat next to me on the couch. When Josh sat next to me, I put my arms around him in a huge hug and gave him a gentle kiss.

"See? Family. See, puppy? Family…friend. This is family," I repeated over and over.

Josh held me and watched quietly as nine pounds of frenzy barked at him. Eventually, the puppy quieted down into little yips and murmurs. Vibrating with energy, he walked across my lap and looked up into Josh's face.

"Hey, buddy," Josh said.

A stern bark informed Josh who the boss was (hint: it wasn't Josh). I couldn't help but laugh at the little dog's spirit. He was certainly a little firecracker, straight out of the inner city, ready to stand up for himself and his new favorite person, me.

As introductions go, it was a little rocky, but by the end of the night, Josh had passed muster and was allowed to rub the puppy's head and scratch his back. Still, every time I got up to use the restroom or walk into the kitchen, the dog would launch himself over the back of the couch in a desperate attempt to keep me from getting too far out of sight.

"Whoa!" Josh said.

"See? Like I said, he's already bonded with me. Big time."

We let the puppy out for the final time that night and watched as he tore down the walkway next to our house. Stopping and dancing around, he broke into a crazy run that is so typical of Bostons.

"Oh my God," breathed Josh.

"I know. Just like Briggs." It was heart-wrenching to watch the mini-Briggs run around and do all the same things Briggs did.

When we went to bed that night, I looked over at the rescue pup as he sat in Briggs' small crate that we'd pulled from the closet. Whimpering, he stared at me.

"Not happening, bucko."

Sighing, he laid down with his head on his paws.

"What are you going to do with him tomorrow?" Josh asked, concerned because we had a memorial service to attend in the morning, followed by a long day of flyer-hanging.

"I have no idea."

Day 17

CHOKING SOBS WOKE ME; IT took a moment to realize they were my own. I was struggling to breathe. Gut-wrenching, deep cries tore their way out of my body. I covered my mouth and tried to be quiet, but the bed shook with my emotion. I heard the puppy whimpering, and I felt the bed dip as Josh rolled over and put his arms around me.

"Baby?"

"I -- I don't know what to do. I don't know how to do this. I can't. I can't keep this dog. There's no way I can stay focused on Briggs and save this dog too."

After a series of unattractive hiccups, I wiped the tears from my face in a losing attempt to calm myself. It was hopeless, though, for I simply could not stop the flow of tears.

"Do you want me to take him to the Humane Society?" Josh asked. It was an option I didn't want to consider.

Crying, I shook my head. No.

The whimpering from the floor grew louder, but I couldn't bear to look at the puppy, knowing we were deciding his fate.

"How about we keep him for a few days and see if we can find any owners? I thought that was the plan," Josh said.

I nodded. I couldn't talk. I couldn't stop crying.

Josh pulled me to him and comforted me.

"Maybe you need a good cry. You haven't since Briggs was stolen…not really anyway. You know that, right?"

I nodded, acknowledging his statement; I hadn't told anyone about my tears in the bathroom earlier that week. Josh's beard scratched my shoulder as he held me, and I tried to concentrate on regulating my breathing. I didn't know how to convey my feelings to him. What I did know was that the new dog had bonded to me, and I couldn't bear to break his heart. But I wasn't ready to accept that yet. I needed to keep my wall up, or else I would let Briggs down. There was no "save and nurture new puppy" portion to our relentless campaign.

"Call that girl at Central Bark and see if she'll take the puppy for the day, and we'll figure out what to do tonight. How does that sound?" Josh asked, his words slurring with sleepiness.

Nodding, I breathed deeply, trying to pull myself back together. A few minutes later, I called Jess, the owner of Central Bark Menomonee Valley, and explained our predicament.

She readily agreed to take the puppy for the day.

"Girl, you sure it isn't that time of the month or something? You're a wreck!" Jess laughed at me, trying to break the tension and make me smile. It worked, sort of.

Smiling weakly, I let her know I'd be there shortly. I then gathered the puppy up, put him through the rigors of the morning feed-poop-walk routine, and then proceeded to get dressed.

Wearing bright colors as requested by my friend, Chuck, for his sister's funeral, I could see that the poppy red of my shirt highlighted the pallor of my skin and the large circles under my eyes. With a shrug, I dismissed it. Makeup could only cover so much.

Driving to Central Bark turned out to be more emotional than I had anticipated. The puppy wouldn't leave my lap and cried the entire time. Doing what I could to reassure him, I promised him that we'd only be apart for a few hours and that I'd be back to pick him up that night. Uttering soothing, nonsensical words, I carried him into Central Bark.

From behind the brightly colored desk, Jess let out an exclamation. A lover of Bostons, she couldn't believe how tiny and cute the little gray one was.

"Wow! I've never seen one that color before."

I explained to her that he was pretty bonded to me already and might have some issues with separation anxiety.

She laughed a bit and dismissed me.

"He's a puppy. He'll be okay!"

Promising to be back before four o'clock, I left without looking back.

It was one of those perfect, early summer days, and the sun shone as we drove to the memorial service. Julie, Chuck's sister, had died that week, and we were there to support Chuck and to help him through the loss of a sister he dearly loved. I hadn't known Julie, but Chuck had told me of her deep love of animals, as well as her infectious love of humor and a good joke. I hurt for my friend, yet it seemed like just another unwelcome layer to my pain.

Josh and I walked into a beautiful, white Episcopalian church. Stark in contrast to many overly ornate churches, this one had huge, clear, antique glass-paned windows that ran the length of the room. It was white inside, almost sterile, with little ornamentation. The message of the min-imalistic, plain décor was simple: all who stepped through those doors were there to celebrate the simplicity and beauty of life.

Sitting in a wooden pew toward the back, I fought back tears as I watched my friend and his family honor the sister they had loved so dearly. Trying to maintain my compo-sure, I stared out of the huge window to my left. A beauti-ful tree, situated directly outside the window, waved its leaves delicately in the wind. I watched the sun dancing through the bright green leaves, a melody of light and col-or; the beauty of it stinging my eyes. I prayed furiously as I sat there, asking God, Julie, the lover of animals, and any other spirit guides that cared to listen.

"Please. Please help. I can't take this much more. I simply can't. I need your help." Focusing on the tree, I repeated this over and over. "Please. Please help."

As the service came to a close with the rousing song, "I don't wanna work. I just wanna bang on my drums all day!" The song shook the mood and turned the memorial into a celebration. Suddenly, everyone's bright wardrobe made sense.

Squeezing my hand tightly, Josh pulled me to offer our condolences to Chuck. We explained that we couldn't stay; we had to use our day to put up flyers. Chuck, a strong supporter of the Briggs search, hugged us and wished us luck.

Emotionally exhausted, and it's only noon, I thought.

After that, Josh and I split up for the day. He was finally going to repair the brakes on my car using his co-workers' tools.

When I kissed him goodbye, he held me for an extra long time and said, "I love you."

"You too," I said. Taking a deep breath, I moved on to my plan for the day.

My friend Kristine had agreed to meet me at El Rey, a Hispanic grocery store on the South Side. We planned to set up shop with a folding table and chairs and try to capture as much attention as we could.

The day had grown hotter, and I crankier, as I waited for Kristine to meet me. Another beautiful day, and I was out hanging flyers. Pushing my heavy hair off of my neck,

I went to greet Kristine at her car and helped her with the table and chairs.

"Let's ask the manager to make sure it's okay, just so we don't get yelled at," Kristine suggested.

As we walked inside, we saw that the food carts were congregated around the entrance and exit to the store, so we'd need to find another spot for our table. I noticed an area by the entrance and exit to the parking lot and pointed it out to Kristine. It was a perfect spot to get attention. After speaking with the manager, who was exceptionally kind, we were able to set up our table in the spot that we had scoped out.

I mentioned to Kristine that we surely would have gotten much more hassle had we gone to a chain grocery store, with all their rules, regulations, and red tape. Loving local stores and their ability to make quick decisions, I was happy that we were able to set up our table with no fuss.

Having considered in advance what our sign should say, I had printed a large neon sign in both English and Spanish. Huge rewards were offered. Our desperation had made us up the ante. My hope was that it would catch people's eyes as they drove in and out of the lot.

The next three hours dragged on. Kristine's enthusiasm and willingness to chase people down in the parking lot to hand them flyers was a huge help. Already at an emotional low, I was having a hard time fighting for people's attention.

One man approached and asked us, in Spanish, about my dog. He appeared to be well off, and his concern was clear. Even more so, we noticed that he seemed like the type who's able to "take care of things." Saying as much, he walked away and pulled out a cell phone.

"Interesting," we both said, taking notice of the gentleman.

"It's better than the assholes who completely ignore us as we try to hand them the flyer," Kristine noted.

That was true, for we'd pleaded with many, but the language barrier, or indifference, had them turn their backs on us.

"Some of these people worry me," I mentioned to Kristine.

"Like the crack addict who keeps circling us?" Rolling her eyes, Kristine gave him the death glare.

"Yes. He's particularly annoying, especially when he asked if we'd go home with him."

A minute later, Annmarie called.

"Tricia, I have great news for you! Remember me telling you about my brother who lives in Seattle? Well, he's a ghost-hunter. I know how crazy that sounds, but he's the head of some paranormal society out there, and they're going to have a show on A&E this year."

Her voice hummed with excitement.

Listening and squinting against the heat of the sun, I encouraged her to continue. I remembered that she had mentioned that her whole family had psychic abilities.

"Well, he called me today and asked me what's wrong. He never does that, and we don't talk very often. He literally could feel how upset I am and called me up. I explained to him the whole story of Briggs and how Kirk and I had gotten involved. Understanding quickly, he told me he has two friends who are animal communicators and would be happy to help for free. How great is that? Are you okay with that?"

I've always believed there is more out there than we know, and I wholeheartedly believe in the ability of some people to tap into other senses.

"Yes, beyond okay! What do you need from me?"

"Forward me as much information as you can about what you know from the day he was stolen. I should be home in an hour or two and by my computer, and I'll email it to him then."

I agreed quickly, and then happily hung up, glad to have more strong people on my side. I would use all forces at my disposal, crazy as they might otherwise seem.

I relayed the conversation to Kristine, and she agreed with me that it was time to pack up. We had been at El Rey for hours, and I was starting to worry about the rescue puppy. I snapped a few pictures for the Facebook page and gratefully thanked Kristine; her strength had helped to keep me sane throughout the day. Doing this alone would have been a nightmare, if not impossible.

Leaving El Rey, I idly contemplated whether we'd given a flyer to the man who had taken Briggs, or perhaps to a family member of his. In any case, I hoped we'd made our presence known in that community.

I hoped we'd given the message loud and clear: "We're here. We aren't going anywhere. We can get even more obnoxious than this. We aren't scared of you, and we will continue to be a thorn in your side until you give Briggs back."

Bolstered by the good news and the progress of the day, I drove to Central Bark, eager to hear how the puppy had fared.

"Hey, Jess. How'd he do?" I asked as I entered the front room.

A *thud* shook the half-door that separated her office from the desk. Accompanied by hysterical crying and scratching, the *thuds* grew louder.

"Um, you weren't kidding when you said he's bonded to you," Jess said as she reached through the door to pick the rescue puppy up.

Squirming hysterically, he dropped from her hands and rushed to me. Scrambling and scratching at me, he twisted and turned and pawed at my legs in a desperate attempt to climb my legs and be closer to me.

"Whoa! Calm down, buddy. I'm here, just like I told you I would be." I picked him up and cradled him close.

He instantly calmed down. Licking my face, he gazed around serenely, an entirely different creature from the hysterical monster he'd been just moments before.

I noticed that he was sporting a dapper new blue collar. Admiring it, I thanked Jess.

"I just wanted to rid him of any reminders of his old place. Figured it might have a bad smell or energy for him."

I thanked her again and asked her how he did.

"Well, I took him to get his vaccinations, as he couldn't be around the other dogs if he wasn't vaccinated. I hope you don't mind."

Understanding, I thanked her.

Continuing on, Jess told me, "It was truly the funniest thing. I kind of blew you off when you said he was bonded to you because…well, for the most part, puppies love everyone. But then he did something today that no other dog has ever done on my watch. When you left, he freaked, ran into my office, leaped on top of the desk, put his paws against the window, and watched you leave. In all my time here, I've never seen a dog do that."

Hearing that was like a knife to my gut. How could I possibly re-home a dog that's bonded to me like that? I knew, with 100 percent certainty, that giving him up would break this little dog's heart. He was a fighter, and I was his final choice for safety. How could I let him down?

With my heart aching, I cradled him in my lap as we drove home. I didn't know what to do. This was my low, my rock bottom. My energy was tapped. I didn't know how to do what I was doing anymore. Feeling fiercely protective, while at the same time hating that I was considering how to give him up, I squeezed the puppy close.

"Briggs. I am not giving up on you."

Saying it out loud helped to strengthen my resolve.

I'm smarter than this, I thought. I can figure out a way to save both. I just need to be stronger. While talking myself up and simultaneously criticizing myself for being a wimp, I thought about our next moves.

As I carried the rescue pup to our front door, I witnessed joy in its purest form; he was ecstatic that we were returning to the same house. Squirming and dancing in front of the door, his little paws lifted and twisted as he emitted yelps of joy at our front door.

"Whoa!" What else could I say? The dog had picked his home, even if I wasn't yet sure how to make it work. Unlocking the door amidst joyous yelps, I felt my phone buzz in my pocket. Checking the screen, I saw that Annmarie was calling me back.

"Tricia, are you sitting down?"

"Um, no…but I can be."

Annmarie explained that she hadn't gotten home yet to forward my email on to her brother. Since she was a little behind the times and didn't use a smartphone, she had to get to an actual computer to forward an email.

"Well, you're not going to believe this, Tricia, but my brother just called." All but hysterical, Annmarie's voice was cracking with excitement.

My heart started pounding faster. Did they know where Briggs is?

"Seriously. I am still on my way home. I haven't sent him anything, but he called me and told me his friend called him and said, 'I know where Briggs is.'"

I almost dropped the phone as my heart dropped into my stomach. Holy shit! But wait… How could this person in Seattle even know Briggs' name? Annmarie's brother didn't even have the information yet to send on to her, so how could she know? I was baffled.

"Keep going," I coaxed, trying to breathe slowly.

"I couldn't believe it either. He hasn't even called her yet! She told my brother, 'Be careful about how you tell the owners this because they're not going to want to hear it.'"

"What!?" Pain shot through me. Tense, I waited. I didn't know if I'd be able to bear what I was about to hear.

"No, just listen. The animal communicator went on to say that Briggs has found a new home. He was in a really, really bad place and was treated horribly, but he is happy now, with a young couple in their thirties. He's deeply bonded with the female, completely in love with her. He stresses that he will not go back to his old home and that nobody can make him. He says if someone forces him to leave, he will try to go back to where he is now. He was crated by the bed this morning and desperately wanted to be up by the female. He was playing with puppies all day today, got his vaccinations, and is gray and white, about four months old. And he was given a new blue collar today."

As I stared numbly down at the rescue puppy at my feet, his new blue collar shining brightly against his gray fur, dizziness struck me. I shook my head, as if to clear it. Her words took hold and emotion slammed into me.

"She was talking about the rescue dog! Oh my God, Annmarie!"

"Oh my God!" Annmarie screamed on the other end of the phone, echoing my amazement at the clarity of the vision, albeit for the wrong dog.

Annmarie went on to say that the animal communicator stressed that the rescue puppy hadn't been stolen by Jason. The puppy didn't want to go back, however, because he was home now and loved the female deeply.

He's home now? Shaking, I had a hard time holding on to the phone.

"He has a new blue collar on. He got it today while I was at El Rey. He was vaccinated when he was at Central Bark and got to play with puppies, and he was crated by the bed this morning. He cried because he wanted to come up."

Annmarie hadn't known any of that. I hadn't spoken with her since she asked me hours earlier to email her information about Briggs.

"Shut up! Oh my God! This is just…incredible," she said, amazed.

Thanking Annmarie, I stammered with as much force as I could, "If she can do that, describe his day in full like that, tell her to find Briggs. She has to find Briggs."

Annmarie agreed to call her brother back, but cautioned me that it might take some time and that she had no idea when I'd get a response from the communicator.

Breathing hard, I hung up and looked down at the rescue dog standing at my feet, and staring up at me with complete and utter trust in his eyes. His little tail wiggled uncontrollably.

Shit. I finally acknowledged what I'd known from the first moment I'd seen a picture of Jason holding him. This dog was ours. I was pretty sure that was why I'd been crying so horribly that morning. Somehow, I'd already decided that he was ours and absolutely hated myself for considering re-homing him.

"So you're home now, huh?"

The wiggling went into overdrive, and he rolled over on his back, cute as could be.

"Uh-huh. So you're a hustler. Don't forget that I've got your number." I smiled down at him.

The most crucial part of the revelation for me was that the puppy wasn't stolen; he'd simply been in a bad home. Mulling that over, I realized it made me significantly more confident in my decision to keep him.

"Okay, buddy. If nobody claims you over the next few days, you can stay."

Smiling, I leaned over and scratched his stomach. He writhed in joy on the kitchen floor. When the front door swung open and Josh walked in, the rescue puppy barked like crazy and ran over to meet/attack him. He still couldn't seem to decide if he was happy to see Josh or ready to protect me from him.

Josh looked at me.

"*What* happened?"

Shock must have been apparent on my face.

"Um, wow. Where do I begin?" Still absorbing the news from the animal communicator, I filled Josh in on my day.

His eyes met mine as I told him about Annmarie's latest phone call. Focusing on the blue collar, his eyes widened with shock.

"I know," I murmured.

"Wow. Just…wow. That's some shit, Tricia. That is some crazy shit." Josh paced the kitchen, still staring at the blue collar on the rescue dog.

"I know!" The thoughts were scrambling in my brain. Deciding not to delve too deeply into the how of the matter, I simply accepted it for what it was.

"So is this *our* dog now?" Josh asked, cutting right to the heart of it.

"Maybe. I kinda think he's home now, but we need to take it day by day. This is too much for me right now."

"Yeah, I don't need you driving yourself crazy nursing this dog to health on top of finding Briggs," Josh said, worried.

It sounded somewhat cold, but I knew where he was coming from. It's hard to watch someone you love work herself to the bone over something. I also knew that it killed Josh that his odd work hours and obligations meant that he couldn't be as involved in the search as I was. I couldn't blame him for that. He was my rock through it all.

"Let's just see what the weekend holds. We can't do anything with him anyway. Tomorrow is Sunday," I suggested. Really though, I just wanted another day to think.

"Okay, but this is just crazy. Seriously. Do you think the animal communicator will conjure up more information on Briggs? Is that what they do? Conjure?" Josh asked with a quizzical expression on his face.

"Um, undetermined." I laughed a little. "Can you feel it? The energy is rolling," I said to Josh.

It was true. The entire day had been that way. Still, this day was different, and there was something specific about it. From the memorial service to the psychic, the energy was palpable.

"I have goosebumps," Josh said, agreeing.

"This is good. Something good is happening."

Josh had to go help his friend move some furniture, but he promised to be back quickly. He didn't want to leave me again.

"Okay, okay, okay." I wandered aimlessly in circles in the kitchen, trying to process. Tapping my fingers on my jeans, I just let the thoughts circle in my head. So many pieces to the puzzle. How does one know which is the right direction to pursue? When my phone rang, I sighed and reached for it.

"Hi. Um, is this the woman with the stolen Boston?"

"Yes. What can I do for you?" Ready to dismiss the call, I idly looked down at the rescue on the floor; he was nibbling on my shoe, content as can be.

"I was out walking my dog and saw a Boston tied up outside a house. I'm around the corner right now. Here's the address. I can wait for you if you want."

I looked down at the rescue dog.

"Let's roll."

Luckily, the address was off of Brady Street, only about a five-minute drive from our home. Pulling into an empty spot, I saw a young man on the sidewalk with his dog. I got out and took the puppy with me on his leash.

"Hey, are you the one who called me?" I said.

"Yes." He pointed out the house where he'd seen the dog and offered to wait for me.

Okay, I think I'll just walk the rescue puppy down the sidewalk and look like any other person on the street with their dog, I decided. Then it dawned on me: *of course.* This was how I can use the rescue dog to help save Briggs. He would be my partner in crime. Anytime I receive a call about a Boston terrier sighting, I could simply go to that block and walk my dog. It was so brilliantly simple.

I walked the rescue slowly past the yard. There was a wall of bushes, and the house was set far back from the street. I saw a young couple on the porch and a Boston tied up in the yard, but I could tell from the sidewalk that it wasn't Briggs. I stopped and effusively thanked the young man for contacting me. Not everyone would have waited to see if it was Briggs or not, and I appreciated this kind stranger's support.

The man on the porch stood up.

"Hey, is that another Boston? Come on up!"

I thanked the guy on the street again and slowly walked up to the porch. The couple, in their mid-thirties, rose to greet me. I could see that the woman was hugely pregnant. She wore a funky haircut and a cool housedress; I admired the mama-to-be's style. The guy, somewhat familiar looking, was super friendly and introduced me to their Boston terrier, Zoe. The little spitfire and the rescue dog immediately started tearing around the yard.

I introduced myself and explained why I was stalking their yard.

"Oh yeah! We've seen the posters everywhere! We're so sorry for your loss."

The couple, Matt and Kelly, were both avid dog lovers, and regularly walked and biked much of the city. As I talked with them, I learned that they'd both been watching, sharing, and looking out for Briggs. They told me they'd been stopped frequently by people checking to see if Zoe was, in fact, Briggs. They didn't seem to mind being stopped, as it only meant people were paying attention to my flyers and trying to keep an eye out for our dog. We laughed and suggested t-shirts for the Boston terrier owners of the city that read, "No, this is not Briggs."

"Wanna hear something really crazy?" Still reeling from what Annmarie had told me about the animal communicator, I filled them in.

"Holy shit." Matt said.

"My thoughts exactly."

I enjoyed the peacefulness of their yard and was happy to let the rescue play with another dog for a little while — until he ran through their freshly planted flowers. Apologizing, I dragged him back.

Remarkably cool, they offered to help in any way they could — even though their baby girl, Mili, was to be born any day. It was nice to spend time with another couple who owned a Boston and who had been involved, unbeknownst to us, in the campaign to find Briggs.

As the sun began to set, the puppy and I made our way home. Mentally reviewing the day, I realized I'd somehow transitioned from exhausted to revved up. Something was happening. I felt it, knew it. Again, the energy was palpable, like static in the air. Too many people were looking, watching, praying, and involved for Briggs to go unfound forever. I had to wonder — what would be the final push?

In a weird way, it was almost as if others felt it as well. That night, I received phone calls from people I had not spoken with for years. Repeating the story of my day over and over, I could feel the energy increasing.

My mom called to see how I was doing, and I could hear the concern in her voice as I told her about my day.

"Just know that you've done everything you could for Briggs, Tricia. I don't know anyone else who would have pushed as hard as you and Josh have. I'm proud of you."

"Thanks, Mom." I knew she thought I needed to ease back, and she was worried for me. If she only knew the half of what I've done, I thought.

That night, Josh and I had a somewhat celebratory cocktail with dinner. We were excited about the animal communicator and proud of our hard work. We were making a difference. People were noticing and caring.

In the throes of one of biggest political conflicts in recent years, all eyes were on Milwaukee and our governor recall election that was to happen the following week. That event was groundbreaking in itself and had severely divided Milwaukee — a city already suffering from crippling segregation. The fact that our dog had made an impact and was pulling people together in the midst of one of the most heated political events to strike the State simply amazed us.

We will find Briggs. We have to.

Exhausted, slightly tipsy, and somewhat content, we put the puppy to bed and curled up together, spent and done.

Day 18

6:00 AM.

My phone.

My damn phone. Again.

Fumbling for it, I missed the call. I squinted and peered at the screen, none too happy to see that it had been from an unavailable number. I also quickly noticed that I'd already missed several calls and that there were several voicemails waiting for me.

Quietly, I rolled away from Josh and turned the volume down on my phone so I could listen to the messages. As was becoming par for the course, some were nonsense. I rolled my eyes and looked at the rescue in his crate. He looked at me questioningly, his head cocked to one side.

The next voicemail was from a man that had left a similar voicemail the week before: "This is Thomas Ardison. I have information on your dog. Call me." Sighing, I deleted the message. We had already played that game with Mr. Ardison a week ago. I'd received a similar message and when I returned the call, a different man had answered, one who'd gotten very angry with me. Fun stuff.

Furious, I looked at all the missed calls. Are you kidding me? I thought. It's Sunday morning. Leave us alone. I was so sick of people messing with us. In desperate need of more sleep, I turned my ringer off for the first time ever.

Two hours later the doorbell rang.

Waking suddenly, Josh and I looked at each other. Was that the doorbell? At eight thirty on a Sunday morning? Confused, and unsure if the doorbell really had rung, we waited to see if it would ring again. Silence answered us.

Groggy, I agreed to go check it out. I wanted to take the rescue puppy out anyway since he was still young enough that bladder control had yet to be mastered.

Josh, not a morning person due to his second shift schedule, murmured, "Okay," and rolled back over.

I grabbed my phone, threw on a sweatshirt, picked up the puppy and went downstairs. I opened the door, squinting into the sunshine. The music from the church next door serenely greeted me.

Our side walkway was empty, but I was on high alert. My senses were tingling. I put the puppy down to potty, pulled my phone out, and started listening to voicemails. More crap, more crap, more crap.

But then: "Hi. This is the church next door. Your dog walked into church this morning. Please call us immediately."

180

As the words registered, I simply started running. I ran backward, forward, stopping, stalling, and almost tripping as I scooped up the rescue dog. Confused and shocked, he yipped at me. In my pajama shorts and hoodie, I raced down the steps and onto the sidewalk. I looked both ways, frozen. I had wanted the moment to come so badly, yet I had no idea what to do. I simply could not believe what was happening. I spotted the gardener in front of the church next door.

Hysterical, I raced to him, "Do you have my dog?!"

Jumping up, he gestured excitedly with his shovel.

"Your neighbor is holding him. Your neighbor has him. He's home!"

Almost dropping the rescue dog, I turned and stumbled. Frozen, I didn't know if I should run inside first or go get Briggs first. My mind, usually so quick to process, failed me.

Josh! The thought registered. I turned and ran back to our front door and slammed it open.

"He's back! He's back! He's back!" The words tore from deep within — a dream being realized.

I had to see Briggs. I turned and ran back to the street, the rescue puppy jostling under my arm, my heart pounding, knowing that Josh would be close behind.

I will never forget that moment.

Our neighbor must have heard my screams because as I reached the street, I heard their door slam. Two houses down from ours, theirs was a typical walk-up house, with steps leading up to their porch from the sidewalk.

I held my breath and stopped. I couldn't comprehend what I would do if it wasn't Briggs in their arms. I knew they had to have the right dog. They wouldn't lie to me about this. This couldn't be another mix-up. This had to be him. It just had to be.

I was unable to take another step. Vaguely, I could hear Josh pounding down the steps behind me.

And then I saw him. Briggs, our baby. There he was, being carried down the steps, his sweet brown eyes boring into mine.

Oh. My. God.

Running without knowing it, I threw the rescue puppy at my neighbor and grabbed Briggs.

Briggs.

Ecstatic, he licked the tears from my face as I buried my face in his neck. I could feel him. I could feel the weight of him in my arms. He was real. I held him — heart-to-heart. He licked and licked my face. I couldn't look up. I just held and rocked him.

He was safe.

My emotions were whirling so fast that I couldn't even process. My skin felt hot, my breath coming in small gasps.

Dazed, I handed Briggs off to Josh, and then just stood there, staring at my husband. He was standing on the sidewalk in loose, thrown-on shorts and no shirt, holding Briggs, with a completely stunned look on his face. I will never forget that image. It was as if his emotions were taking too long to process and catch up to his face. Finally,

finally, I saw a smile crack open on his face. Locking eyes, we both just started to laugh.

As people started to pour from their houses and surround us, I finally noticed that there was some hysteria going on next to me.

"Um, I think he wants you." My neighbor handed the squealing rescue puppy back to me.

In all the commotion, I'd completely forgotten about him.

"Oh shit, yes. Thank you. Do you want to meet your brother?" I held the rescue dog and gestured to Josh to put them both down together.

Setting them both on the grass in front of our house, we watched in amazement as Briggs immediately bounced into the play position, and they began to tear around the yard, chasing each other ecstatically.

"Wow! It's almost like they really are brothers," someone in the crowd said.

"They are." I said, smiling.

Deliriously happy, I finally looked around at the laughing crowd.

"Can someone please tell us what happened?" I asked.

It wasn't until then that I realized that we didn't even know how Briggs had gotten home, aside from the voicemail telling me he'd walked into the church, and Josh didn't even know that much.

The story unraveled from various sources as everyone chimed in.

"He was just sitting outside the church, waiting patiently!"

"The gardener brought him inside!"

"The pastor asked if he was that stolen dog and held him up to the entire congregation. He got a standing ovation."

On that comment I looked up and started laughing. I bent over and laughed my heart out. Our dog had been held up to the congregation; the prodigal dog returned. I pictured a ray of light piercing the stained-glass windows, shining onto him as he was raised over the congregation. How entirely perfect, I thought. Of course that's how he'd return to us — naturally with a healthy flair for drama. Briggs couldn't just wait at our door like he'd been taught to do. Our dog had to be raised before an adoring crowd.

Josh and I simply couldn't stop laughing.

Stupidly happy, we kept capturing tidbits of the story. The gardener had found him and kept him inside, giving him water, until the pastor held him to the congregation. Our neighbor heard of it and, knowing Briggs, took him in.

I told everyone about the phone calls that morning and how I'd turned off the ringer in exhaustion and frustration. We speculated that whoever had taken him had grown so frustrated with me not answering the phone that they simply dropped him at our house, where Briggs then waited.

But the time for theories was later. Now was the time to celebrate. After many hugs and tearful congratulations, we wandered back inside with our dogs.

Our dogs. Plural.

Dazed, Josh and I watched as Briggs immediately went to his toys, grabbed one in his mouth, ran over to us, and dropped it at our feet. He was fine, totally fine, and not hurt at all. He hadn't had to walk fifteen miles home, and he wasn't dirty, scarred, or beaten up. He was full of energy, clean, and ready to play.

Not even knowing who to contact first, I just stared at Briggs with pure happiness as the rescue puppy tried to pull the toy from his mouth.

Josh turned to me and pulled me close.

"You did it, baby. We did it, but you extra did it."

Laughing and burying my face in his neck, I trembled with joy.

"We did this."

Happily watching the dogs play, I called my parents as Josh picked up the phone to call his.

An 8:30 a.m. phone call on Sunday warranted both of my parents picking up the phone from different extensions in their house.

"He's back. He's home safe!" I exclaimed, watching as Josh repeated the same words on his phone to his parents.

"What!?" both of my parents stumbled over each other to speak. When I relayed the story, they shouted for joy.

"I have to tell you, I was pretty sure he was a goner," my dad related to me gravely.

"I know, Dad, but I appreciate you refraining from expressing that while he was missing."

I ended the conversation with them, and then called Kristine.

"He's home! I think El Rey may have done it."

Sobbing, she congratulated me.

Meghan was next, and her cries of joy shook me. The other Megan, our daily warrior that we'd not known prior to it all, got a message. She was riding in a bike race that day, wearing a Briggs flyer on her jersey. I knew she'd be ecstatic to hear the news after her race. Matt and Carrie were instantly informed, and then we turned to the rest of the Briggs community.

When I called Annmarie's place, Kirk answered the phone and told me she'd had a difficult night and had gone back to sleep. I knew that the stress of the prior day had worn on her, and she felt things deeply.

"He's home," I said.

"No."

"He's home!" I quickly explained the story, and he promised to wake Annmarie.

As I continued my calls, my email beeped with pictures from our neighbor who'd snapped several pictures of us with Briggs from his phone, so now I would have something to post to Facebook.

Facebook! I had forgotten for a moment about our Facebook page. Holy shit would this make everyone's Sunday morning, I thought.

Uploading a picture of me burying my face in Briggs' neck as he licked my face, the only caption I could think of was, "SAFE! SAFE! SAFE!" That seemed to be the quickest way to sum things up.

My phone rang, and I heard Annmarie's tremulous voice on the other end.

"He's back? Is he really back?"

Excitedly, I filled her in and promised to bring them both over later in the day.

"This has renewed my faith in humanity," she said, and I could feel Annmarie's joy through the phone.

As the news spread, our phones exploded with texts, calls, and email alerts. I grabbed a charger, plugged my phone in, and ignored it for a moment while I checked Facebook, only to find hundreds of likes, comments, and shares.

The unraveling aftermath was simply amazing. To say that more than one person's faith in humanity was restored would do the situation no justice.

As a local police officer who walked our neighborhood nightly with his dogs said to me, "You understand that this simply doesn't happen. I'm not even saying less than 1 percent. I'm saying .00001 percent."

And he was absolutely right.

This doesn't happen. At least not often.

And not even rarely.

We weren't simply an exception. We were *the* exception.

We could speculate for years over what really happened, where Briggs really had been.

As far as what I believe, I think a man stole him for his kids, like the psychic had predicted. I think a woman close to this man, perhaps a wife, girlfriend, mother, or grandmother (the old woman Briggs stayed with during the day?) found out about it, went to the man, and said, "What did you *do?*" I think that woman forced him to return Briggs, without asking for a reward. The fact that it happened on a Sunday, during a church service, certainly gave a redemptive quality to the whole ordeal. After all, he simply could have driven Briggs outside the city, opened the car door, and kicked him out, problem solved.

But that isn't what happened.

We had pushed hard enough, and now he was back. Someone finally said, "Enough." To this day, we don't know what happened. And that's fine with us.

What I do know is that from now on, I'll pay more attention to people who ask for help. Why? Because I know what it's like to feel helpless. Because ultimately, that is what saved Briggs: a community of people who decided to care about a small dog, stolen from a porch, on a sunny day in May.

Maybe we all needed a happy ending.

After

THE SUN GENTLY PLAYED IN the trees as we pulled into the driveway at my parents' home on pristine Elkhart Lake, Wisconsin. My parents opened the door, jubilantly spilling out in their excitement to see the dogs.

We had always loved taking Briggs to the lake. He loved the freedom of running around, sticking his nose under trees and into roots, and barking at the fish in the water. Now, with two dogs, the excitement was doubled. Laughing, we watched as they raced down one side of the house and zipped up the other.

Pulling us into hugs, my parents told us how proud they were of us, and that they didn't know many people who would have pushed so hard to get their dog back. Happiness flooded me as I watched Briggs and the newly renamed rescue puppy, Blue, bark at each other.

"Let's go down to the lake!"

I couldn't wait to sit on the pier and dip my feet in the water, soak up the sun, and enjoy a well-deserved and way overdue day to relax. My parents' house was situated on a large hill that overlooked the lake. As we got to the bottom, Briggs ran ahead and started tearing around by the lower deck and digging behind a tree.

"Is he...did he find it?" my dad asked.

"Find what?"

All of a sudden, Briggs poked his head out triumphantly, all but grinning with his prize — a dilapidated flip-flop, hanging from his mouth. The flip-flop had floated to shore the summer before, and Briggs had claimed it as his own. Briggs knew he wasn't allowed to chew on shoes, but because he'd found that one himself, it was his prize. He had guarded it all summer long the year before and was ecstatic to find it again.

"I'll be damned," my dad said.

"His flip-flop!" I exclaimed.

"Yes, and you're not going to believe this, but I was cleaning up down here while he was gone, and I picked it up and started to throw it because I didn't want it to upset you and Josh if you saw it without Briggs. I was going to let it float away to another shore, but I stopped. Something stopped me. Even though at the time I was convinced that Briggs was never coming back, I couldn't throw it away, so I hid it behind the tree and under the deck, just in case."

Tears pricked my eyes as I stared at Briggs and the broken flip-flop dangling happily from his mouth.

"Thanks, Dad."

Faith is a strong word. My dad hadn't believed Briggs would come home, yet somewhere deep down, his faith made him hesitate to throw away that old shoe-turned-dog-toy.

That's the funny thing about faith — about hope. You just never know. Things may not work out the way that you expect. And there may not always be a happy ending.

But if you give up, if you walk away, if you turn your back, *if you throw the flip-flop away*, then you give away your faith — in yourself and in others.

I looked at Briggs and Blue and my happy, smiling husband, and I knew we'd all made it happen. One very determined couple and a community of people who had decided they wanted to believe.

To meet Briggs and Blue visit:
www.thestolendog.com.

Alyou
313 580 3028

Oct. 8th 2.5p

Mary Ann
248 421-0939

Made in the USA
Lexington, KY
27 February 2014

30262761R00123